APPLES & ORANGES

Apples & Oranges

In Praise of Comparisons

MAARTEN ASSCHER

Translated from the Dutch by Brian Doyle-Du Breuil

FOUR WINDS
— PRESS —

SAN FRANCISCO

Copyright © 2015 Maarten Asscher
Translation copyright © 2015 Brian Doyle Du-Breuil

N ederlands
letterenfonds
dutch foundation
for literature

The publisher gratefully acknowledges the support
of the Dutch Foundation for Literature.

Originally published in 2013 by Atlas Contact as
Appels en peren. Lof van de vergelijking

Four Winds Press
San Francisco, CA
FourWindsPress.com

ISBN: 978-1-940423-06-7

Cover and interior design by Domini Dragoone
Cover photo © Paul Coles, flickr.com/photos/mr_fujisawa
Distributed by Publishers Group West

For Willem, as *antipasto misto*

CONTENTS

APPLES AND ORANGES

In Praise of Comparisons

On February 21st, 1822, near the Palazzo Ducale in Venice, the Italian writer Silvio Pellico, famous for his play *Francesca da Rimini*, was sentenced to death. Since the Congress of Vienna in 1815, the Austrians had been running the show in Lombardy and Veneto, the northern part of what forty years later was to become a united Italy, and they maintained their authority the hard way, with police interventions and active censorship. The literary and journalistic circles in which Pellico lived and moved were populated with freethinking anti-Austrian liberals, both independence activists and what we would nowadays call 'critical intellectuals'. More or less secret meetings of like-minded individuals were routinely organized, and were soon branded as subversive 'Carbonarism' by the Austrian secret police, which followed up with heightened police readiness from 1819 onwards. Under the leadership of the brilliant Tyrolean jurist Antonio Salvotti, a special commission was established in Venice charged with tracking down, prosecuting, and condemning the participants. Dozens of arrests were made, and Pellico was among those to land in prison after being detained on Friday October 13th, 1820, on suspicion of high treason.

Pellico's death sentence was commuted to fifteen years *carcere duro* and later reduced to seven and a half years, but given the circumstances in which he was obliged to sit out his time – in the dark and dreary dungeons of Spielberg Castle in Moravia – it's nothing short of a miracle that the fragile Pellico managed to survive. His renowned prison memoir *Le mie prigioni* (1832) details the period.

Before being removed by gondola and then by coach to the sinister Spielberg on March 25th, 1822, Pellico was granted permission to write a few letters. He used the opportunity to pen a couple of lengthy missives to his father and an exceptionally groveling word of thanks to the infamous Salvotti, outrageously implausible in its hypocrisy. The same is true for the following passage from a letter dated March 23rd, 1822, addressed to the Sardinian vice-consul in Venice:

> *To the consolation I ask you to convey to my parents, I request in addition that you adjoin the fact of which you are well aware, namely that I have always been treated here with the most generous kindness.*

I find it impossible to read this passage without being reminded of a similar declaration of farewell penned by Sigmund Freud as he was preparing to leave for England with his family, where he was to spend the last years of his life. After the Austrian *Anschluss* of 1938 the Freud family had become surrounded by the exuberant anti-Semitism to which the Austrian and German Nazis had now surrendered themselves as one. Before the authorities would let the elderly Freud go, they insisted that he – like so many others shamelessly harassed into leaving their country – make a statement confirming that the Gestapo had treated him with respect. Freud did indeed sign such a declaration, and in a fit of cynical humor he added the following in his own handwriting:

I can heartily recommend the Gestapo to anyone.

The question is whether we are actually at liberty to draw such a historical parallel, between Pellico's farewell declaration and that of Freud. Pellico was a writer who objected to the foreign occupation of his country, something about which he conversed and corresponded with others; Freud was a Jewish doctor who maintained an extensive international network. Those were their only faults. Both were scandalously treated, a reality both denied in writing in the most incredibly polite terms on the occasion of their forced departure from their homeland. Clearly neither was free to write about the reality of the situation, although from alternative sources we are familiar with the details.

These would indeed appear to be similarities, but the prevailing objection argues that such comparisons are lame, because the historical circumstances in which Pellico was transported to prison by the state police and the historical situation in which Freud was expelled from his country by the secret state police are too different. But what is it that would make drawing this comparison so inappropriate? Would it be morally objectionable? Does it run counter to academic principles? Is the objection based exclusively on the one-hundred and sixteen years that separate the events? On the fact that Austria in 1822 and Austria in 1938 are totally incomparable? So what do we mean when we say that a comparison is 'lame'?

The accusation of lameness is often leveled at comparisons, including those between peoples – Greeks and Turks, for example, or Jews and Palestinians – and books, such as the parallels drawn by American literary critics between *De ontdekking van de hemel* – *The Discovery of Heaven* by Harry Mulisch and the work of Homer and Dante. Those who venture such comparisons are destined to face fierce resistance and will have to fight their corner. The most ingrained resistance tends to be reserved for the historical comparison, and anyone proposing the comparative method is likely to find historical comparison the toughest nut to crack. But let's try our luck.

THE CHRISTMAS 2010 EDITION OF THE DUTCH WEEKLY *Vrij Nederland* published an interview with Job Cohen, leader at the time of the Dutch Labor Party, in which he responded with 'yes' when asked whether present-day Muslims in the Netherlands were being excluded in the same way as the Jews had been at the beginning of the German occupation. His statement drew intense fire from various quarters. Writing in the national daily *de Volkskrant,* writer Joost Zwagerman labeled Cohen's words 'defamatory', while Rotterdam rabbi Raphael Evers – an authoritative spokesman among Dutch Jews – suggested in the *Nieuw Israëlietisch Weekblad* that Cohen's comparison did an injustice both to Muslims and to the history of the Jews in the Netherlands.

Another historical comparison was put to the test a little earlier by Nexus[1] front man Rob Riemen, who in an essay entitled *De eeuwige terugkeer van het fascism – The Eternal Return of Fascism* claimed that the ideas and political movement of Geert Wilders are strongly reminiscent of the early days of fascism. Vigorous rejections followed from both historians and politicians, arguing that such comparisons should not be made because the differences between now and then are too significant.

THE MORE FREQUENT AND VIGOROUS THE OPPOSITION to historical comparison, the more I am convinced that drawing such parallels can be interesting and informative, especially when the comparison is related to contemporary events. Those who make historical comparisons from a present day perspective associate a current feature of the age, which is still happening and thus not yet crystallized, with past events, the course and consequences of which are known to us. While we are still unclear on the future significance of an ongoing reality, the comparison supplies an interpretative, perhaps even cautionary reference to one or more events from the past of which we know the outcome.

---

1. Nexus is an internationally oriented Dutch cultural think tank connected to Tilburg University.

An example: after Bernard Welten, then chief commissioner of the Amsterdam police, publicly stated that he would not enforce the burka ban announced by prime minister Rutte's first cabinet, the country's politicians descended on him in unison, Geert Wilders tweeting at their head: Welten was expected to do his job and enforce the law. But a brief letter to the editor written by a resident of The Hague and published in *NRC Handelsblad* on January 10th, 2011, drew a comparison: 'If we had had a police commissioner like Bernard Welten in 1940-'45, who insisted that the police should not drag Jews from their homes, there may have been a little less suffering and a little less post-war critique of the force.' Lo and behold: a fine example of a historical comparison that ignores the differences and hones in on an issue by way of comparison, thereby communicating a point of view that might otherwise not have been so simple to expose, or at least not with the same succinctness. In short, the inherently selective and simplifying effect of the historical comparison is an uncommonly potent way of making something clear.

But isn't simplification ultimately lethal if we want to acquire a proper understanding of the differences between the past and the present? Not in my opinion. In the aforementioned Job Cohen interview, in which the former mayor of Amsterdam recounts that his mother felt just as excluded at the beginning of the war as he imagined Dutch Muslims today feel excluded, the differences between then and now are as clear as day. The active and systematic exclusion of Jews by the German occupier was followed by round-ups, imprisonments, forced deportations, and intentional, wholesale annihilation. Everyone knows – including Job Cohen himself – that while the comparison with

1940-'45 was apropos, there is nothing to suggest that the same events are likely to present themselves today. Cohen's historical comparison clearly does not state that then and now are the same, rather it signals a parallel between the feeling of exclusion experienced by one group at the beginning of the 1940s and another group in the present day. Those who draw a comparison between Napoleon's Russian campaign and Hitler's Operation Barbarossa don't have to apologize for the countless differences between 1812 and 1941 as long as they do something meaningful and convincing with the parallel they posit. Likewise, Job Cohen should not be criticized for the aspects of his historical comparison that 'fall short'. He should be judged rather on the insight he was able to derive from the comparison, to the extent that he considered it to hold true.

Another advantage of historical comparison is that it promotes the transparency and falsifiability of an argument. Engaging in polemic with implicit claims is much trickier. The majority of historical parallels tend to be implicit, in most instances already locked into the language itself. In my description of the environment in which the Italian Carbonarist Silvio Pellico lived, I spoke about 'freethinking liberals' and 'independence activists'. My interpretation of Carbonarism can be determined immediately on the basis of my choice of words. I could have spoken about 'traitors', 'conspirators', and 'rebels against legitimate Austrian authority'. My terminology alone draws an implicit comparison with other European revolutions and liberation movements. The more explicit I make the comparison, the clearer my position becomes to the reader and the easier it is to call me to account for my interpretation.

A final advantage of historical comparison is its capacity to expose in shorthand how a person approaches a given subject. Cohen's comparison between the position of Muslims in the Netherlands today and that of Dutch Jews at the beginning of the German occupation clearly revealed – and with greater clarity than any contemporary description – the associations, sensitivities, and reference framework with which the prominent Dutch Labor Party executive approached issues of immigration and integration. What you and I think about the background of his 'yes' is irrelevant; the important point is that the comparison grants us an illuminating insight into Job Cohen's moral interior. Those who agree with him are likely to be more receptive to his ideas, those who disagree will be better prepared to challenge him.

In other words: long live historical comparisons, especially when they fall short, as they almost always do. Their limitations are precisely what makes them so interesting and useful. No one has to explain that the Austrian Nazis who were so eager to cooperate with the German Gestapo to expel undesirable elements such as Sigmund Freud are not the same Austrians as those who hunted down the Carbonarists in Northern Italy. And yet, the comparison between 1822 and 1938 articulates the fact that in both cases the police actions were based on unquestioning obedience to an authority and national interest taken to be absolute, and that each of the two victims wrote highly questionable declarations about the treatment they had received at the hands of the police.

What the comparison between these incidents demonstrates is that neither instance is historically unique. It may be that this parallel nourishes a particularly negative image of the Austrian and – if you like – the pan-German police mentality. Alternatively, the comparison might indicate that in both cases there was indeed an awareness of good and evil, but that historical circumstances sometimes weigh more than humanitarian principles. All such arguments and insights can be formulated and discussed thanks to the comparison made.

BY TRADITION, HISTORIOGRAPHY HAS ALWAYS BEEN more preoccupied with distinguishing features than with shared features, more with the specific than the general. One early exception was Plutarch, author of parallel biographies of illustrious Romans and Greeks. However, his primary concern was more prescriptive than historical, intended to encourage his Roman readers to emulate their illustrious Greek counterparts. It was only with the Enlightenment and its more objectified and early modern world view, and thereafter the emergence of the social and economic sciences in the nineteenth century reinforced by nationalistic rivalry between the European nations, that comparison came to be favored as a research model. Sociologist Émile Durkheim and economist-historian Max Weber are particularly noted for their propagation of comparison as an interpretive method. New sorts of historical data, for example in the form of statistics, made previously unthinkable comparisons possible. After the First World War, when historians like Marc Bloch endeavored to determine on the basis of comparative analysis how it was possible, against divergent national backgrounds, for such a large-scale conflict to erupt, 'comparative history' evolved into an independent discipline, resulting in comprehensive surveys like Arnold Toynbee's twelve volume history of the world and studies in which the decline of 'the West' (Oswald Spengler) were described. But in reality, such excessively generalistic studies were a distortion of the comparative perspective because the terms of the comparison were not always specified with equal clarity.

After the Second World War, the comparative perspective continued to flourish. Take the history of the industrial revolution, a subject that would be difficult to cover without an international comparative perspective. At the same time, however, a countermovement was gathering force among historians: comprehensive international meta-histories – with their abundance of generalistic interpretations – made way for 'micro-histories', in which the smallest possible constituent, the strictly particular, was studied as a model for history's grander narratives. Examples here include Carlo Ginzburg's *Il formaggio e i vermi – The Cheese and the Worms*, Emmanuel Le Roy Ladurie's *Montaillou*, and from the Netherlands A.Th. van Deursen's *Het dorp in de polder - The Village in the Polder* about the village of Graft in the seventeenth century.

IN APPROACHING THEIR SUBJECT, MODERN OBSERVERS of art, literature, or history always have a choice between two trajectories: they can generalize, or they can particularize. In other words, they can be deductive or inductive. People like me who enjoy comparisons tend to prefer the particularizing, inductive approach: first explore the unique, and from there move on to the universal. If both terms of a comparison are described with sufficient clarity, it creates two narratives that can be paralleled with one another, and the connections between them can be explored.

The present volume offers the reader a varied collection of pieces in which the comparative perspective is key to the debate. Whether the focus is on history, literature or art, I have sought, sometimes quite explicitly, at other times more implicitly, for a 'stereoscopic' view, like the two slightly differing photographs that together produce a single combined image in a stereoscope. Thanks to the difference between the two photographs, the resulting image acquires depth, a third dimension. My hope, therefore, is that these comparisons, parallels, and juxtapositions will similarly provide depth, and will offer a perspective on remoter truths.

Every historical event, every life, every book, indeed every subject is by definition unique, and as such can only be compared with itself. But since there is little to derive from such a procedure, comparison with other historical events, lives, books and subjects is both necessary and illuminating. No one ever learned much from comparing apples with apples.

A TALE OF TWO SEAS

Kees Fens and Predrag Matvejević

A myriad of books have been supported with loving enthusiasm by their publishers only to find they don't make the
grade in commercial terms. In such instances, the appearance
of the occasional review can offer considerable consolation to
the publisher in question (not to mention the author and perhaps translator), particularly when it gives the stakeholders the
impression that they did the right thing, at least in the opinion
of a few kindred spirits. If the reviews don't materialize, or those
that do are downright negative, then there's little left to do but
harbor a grudge for years and wait for some other chance to
get even. This is what I would like to do with a book entitled
Mediteranski Brevijar (literally 'Mediterranean Breviary'), written
by the Croatian author Predrag Matvejević.

From the moment I got hold of the French Fayard edition (*Bréviaire méditerranéen*, 1992), I was fascinated by this exuberant and irrepressible homage to the sea of seas. Two years after the French edition, Tom Eekman's Dutch translation was published by Meulenhoff on my own instigation under the title *De Middellandse Zee. Een getijdenboek.* The prologue, written by the Italian author Claudio Magris, describes the book as 'masterful, original and brilliant', qualifications with which I heartily agreed and still do.

Anyone trying to imagine what this book by Matvejević might be like should think of a work about the Mediterranean written by an author who represents a timeless amalgamation of Herodotus, Bill Bryson, Pliny the Elder, and Redmond O'Hanlon. The book, in short, is an endeavor to put together a sort of biography of the inexhaustible topography, history, natural and cultural abundance of '*mare nostrum* – our sea', with the maximum curiosity, the maximum craving for detail and the maximum drive for completeness.

Since its original (Serbo-)Croatian publication in 1987, the book has appeared in more than twenty languages. The website of the University of California Press, the book's American publisher, lists it under 'Geography, Classics, Folklore & Mythology, Cultural Anthropology, European Studies, European History, Travel'. This is a meaningful enumeration for two reasons. In the first instance, there has to be something remarkable about a book of little more than two hundred pages that can apparently be relevant to so many different domains at one and the same time. In the second instance, Matvejević's book can itself be seen as 'one big summary', and it is thus appropriate that the publisher's commercial bibliographers maintain such an *enumeratio* in an effort to do justice to its unclassifiable versatility.

My disappointment and surprise were great, therefore, when Kees Fens, a literary critic I admire greatly, completely and utterly demolished Matvejević's book in *de Volkskrant* on June 13th, 1994. I had secretly hoped that he would review it, entirely convinced as I was that it would appeal to him. But the man was unable to find a single good word to say about the book, with the exception of a word of praise for Tom Eekman's translation. In my view, a confrontation between Fens' crushing condemnation and my still sprightly enthusiasm for the book reveals something about 'the Mediterranean': as a mentality, an orientation, perhaps even a quality that people have or don't have.

PREDRAG MATVEJEVIĆ WAS BORN IN 1932 IN MOSTAR, A city that acquired recent renown in Western Europe when the sixteenth century bridge over the river Neretva was destroyed during the 1990s Balkan conflict. Prior to his emigration to France, Matvejević taught French at the University of Zagreb and afterwards, Slavic languages at the Sorbonne in Paris. His existence thus made a 180 degree turn from Eastern Europe to Western Europe. Whatever the East/West significance may be, his book about the Mediterranean confirms him as a European. It won him the *Premio Malaparte* in Italy in 1991, and in the years that followed, the French *Prix du Meilleur Livre Étranger* and the *Prix Européen de l'Essai Charles Veillon*.

The Bosnian city of Mostar is located fifty kilometers inland from the Adriatic coast. One could interpret *Mediterranean Breviary* as a large-scale endeavor to bridge this distance, rooted in a desire to compensate for the Mediterranean's fifty kilometer deficit and still demand a birthright on its shores. Matvejević approaches this in three ways in his book, each corresponding to one of its three parts.

In the first part ('Breviary') he offers a comprehensive phenomenology of the Mediterranean in which he considers the sea's various characteristics and its every phenomenon, great or small: bays, piers, harbormasters' offices, fishing nets, algae, waves, winds, clouds, coasts, lighthouses, tar, figs, olives, sponges, islands, peninsulas, seagulls, river deltas, curses, languages, measures, methods of salt extraction, etc. On the basis of all these characteristics, an ample supply of stories and information floats to the surface. The cities on the Mediterranean coast, for example, did not begin life as villages but actually gave birth to the villages around them. The nature of a harbor, the author informs us, is determined by whether it was formed by a hinterland river or selected from the sea. Why is the Peloponnesus considered a peninsula, he asks, and not Tunisia? Or can we speak of sea migrations by analogy with those of peoples, birds, and fish? And what about the vanity of bays that sometimes pretend to be a sea in themselves, such as the Adriatic, which once bore the – more unassuming – name *Golfo di Venezia*. Or the similarity between lighthouse keepers and monks. Or the fact that the Sea of Marmara is saltier than the Black Sea. All useless facts and questions splendidly foisted upon us by the author.

In part II ('Maps'), Matvejević treats the Med like a cartographical library. We join him as he explores the lives and works of the major and minor mapmakers who have endeavored since time immemorial to capture 'our sea' on paper for the benefit of travelers, fishermen, seafarers, admirals, pirates, and last but not least, the sleuths who forage in our archives and catalogs. He charts islands, for example, that we will never be able to visit because they're not surrounded by sea, but rather they close an imaginary gate: the northern *Ultima Thule* or the western Isles of the Blessed. One special category are the maps we know about only through the descriptions of others. We will never be able to reconstruct their magnificence, evocativeness, and precision. The maps also inspire Matvejević to recount the expeditions, wars, and campaigns of conquest organized by the Phoenicians and Greeks, Venetians and Arabs, Ottomans and Spanish, Carthaginians and Portuguese. How the Arabian cartographers drew their primary meridian through Mecca and located the south ('our' south) above it. How the great cartographers chose the theater and the mirror as their favorite metaphors when depicting the lands and seas of the ancient world: *Theatrum orbis terrarum*, Mirror of Seafaring. And about the centuries old connection between the sea routes and the position of the stars: *Teatro del Cielo e della Terra*. How geography in Antiquity became a critique of the novel; how the great Mercator promoted it to a critique of the imagination; and how Voltaire was ultimately to declare it a critique of the vanity of princes. Matvejević also interweaves his own observations with his archival and cartographical discoveries, sailing past Greek islands on the ship Dodekanesos. He provides a semi-tongue-in-cheek description of a geographer's congress in Amalfi, where a commemorative exhibition of old compass roses was opened in honor of the Russian cartographer Leonid Barov (1881-1957) followed by an opportunity for discussion. This leads him to further digress on the relationship between the development of the compass and the history of the Mediterranean compass rose or wind rose. He closes the second part of his book with the following words: 'The more we know about our sea, the less we look at it with our own eyes; the Mediterranean Sea isn't a sea for the lonely.'

Having dealt with Mediterranean phenomenology and cartography, Matvejević turns in the third part of his book ('Glossarium') to the idiom of the Mediterranean Sea: the words, languages, dialects, and expressions associated with the Mediterranean basin. Just as the author did in going from part I to part II, he continues his argument with different means. His narrative descriptions and anecdotal digressions are now based on the countless names ascribed to the Mediterranean Sea, the multitude of ideas used to describe its individual gulfs, bays, and coves, and their etymological and historical roots. In doing so he not only uses encyclopedias and nautical hand-books, but also ships' logbooks and travel accounts. Together with the author, we lament the loss of the ten volume *Peri limenon* (*On Ports*) by Timosthenes of Rhodes, admiral in the navy of Ptolemy II Philadelphus.

Matvejević helps us compensate for the loss with his com-bination of evocative curiosity and imaginative associations. On the etymological relationship between ports as harbors and ports as doors or gateways, on sunken harbors as necropolises, on maritime cemeteries and their significance as a source of Mediterranean history. And islands, of course, including their historiographical and toponymic associations with classical, medieval, and later figures, up to and including Napoleon, Goethe, Trotsky, D.H. Lawrence, and Lawrence Durrell. This leads to incidental, but no less memorable nuggets of information, like the observation that the less a fish is valued as food the more names it tends to have. The author makes similar observations about the names and functions of herbs and olives, market squares and boulevards, souks and bazaars, weights and measures. This leads in turn to a fine reflection on the temperamental difference between the oriental bazaar and the Latin market. But a couple of pages later we're back to the influence of crickets on the prosody of Hellenistic poetry and the question of which part of a seagull actually touches the surface of the water first: its breast, its claws, its beak, or its wings?

Such matters are important. They can keep you busy as you stare out to sea while the waiter brings you another glass of tea, an ouzo, or a local fig distillate. It's hard to draw conclusions from them, but conclusions aren't really necessary. In truth, and if we are to believe the book, nothing is necessary, but everything is worth studying and thinking about.

MATVEJEVIĆ'S BREVIARY WAS CLEARLY WASTED ON Kees Fens, as is unequivocally evident from his review. At the beginning of his piece he notes that he spent an entire day with the book, but 'didn't achieve perfection'. He diagnoses 'verbal dandruff' on the part of the author, a 'mania for collecting and explaining'. He even opines here and there that he's dealing with parody (without attempting to answer the interesting question: of what might the book be a parody?). He considers the book to be a sort of catalogue, but one that 'means nothing' and affords the reader no – new – insights. The book appears extremely profound, according to Fens, but 'in fact it's almost empty'. In his opinion it doesn't provide any 'real information' and is little more than a 'chain reaction of words'. 'I've rarely read an author,' he concludes admittedly with some wit, 'who allows himself to be towed along by words to such a degree. [...] There appears to be a lot. But if you read carefully there's nothing to read.' Fens explains this by arguing that 'there is an absence of clarity and its associated pedagogical demands'. His final words: 'Matvejević's helmsmanship is the reason why the ship keeps turning on its axis. We never move forward. [...] I was constantly thinking [...] about the end of the journey. In the hope that its uniqueness would dawn on me. But there was no lighthouse up ahead, no beacon, no buoy, no harbor, no quay, no mooring berth. In short: there was nothing to hold on to. Nothing, that is, except the extraordinary talents of the translator Tom Eekman'.

IN CONTRAST TO MY OWN ENTHUSIASTIC READING OF Predrag Matvejević's book, what Kees Fens' brutal critique reveals is not only a difference of taste, of someone who admires a book vis-à-vis someone who detests it. There appears rather to be evidence of an unbridgeable divergence of minds. For Kees Fens, *Mediterranean Breviary* should have had a beginning as well as a middle and an end. More precisely, it should have had an 'outcome' that would have made 'perfection' achievable. Only then would the book have had meaning for him – mindful of the 'pedagogical demands' – and only then would the reader have been granted something to 'hold on to' at the end of the book.

But the very thing that draws me to Matvejević's book and continues to enthrall me is its rambling character, its aimlessness, not its linearity (from beginning to end), but its circularity (rambling as a goal in itself). Its words move forward like waves suggesting a sea in the form of a book. After Fernand Braudel and hundreds of other authoritative histories of the culture, history and geography of the Mediterranean, what's the point of more 'useful information' about 'our sea'? I honestly wouldn't know. But the fact that the inhabitants of Herculaneum didn't swim on their backs or bellies but on their sides, as Erwin Mehl's *Antike Schwimmkunst* (Munich, 1927) informs us, is the kind of unforgettable detail I particularly like to indulge, and of such details Matvejević is a most successful collector. So what inspired the horror that evidently took hold of Fens and refused to let him go for two hundred pages? The answer, it suddenly dawned on me, had to do with the difference between the Mediterranean and the North Sea, with Zandvoort on the North Sea coast, Kees Fens' former hometown, and with the cultural differences that distinguish such a northern seaside resort from the southern reality of the Mediterranean.

IN A COUNTRY LIKE THE NETHERLANDS, WHERE THE tulips line up every year, where the trees serve in the first place as protection against the wind from the sea, and where people think of the sea in terms of tides (and the climate in terms of rain), a book needs to offer something to hold on to, prove its perfection in the space of a day on the basis of the 'useful information' it yields. More than anything else, it has to 'mean something', otherwise it's nothing. Don't forget those 'pedagogical demands'! Kees Fens painstakingly reminds us of these rigid rules and he's right to proclaim them for all to hear, in the Netherlands that is. But in the culture of the Mediterranean, from which this book emerged and into which it immerses itself anew after reading, such practical necessities don't count. A book doesn't need to move from A to B in the Mediterranean. A Mediterranean book writes its own language drawing from the countless alphabets that have come into existence on its shores across the centuries. Instead of mercantile tulip bulbs, the Mediterranean has useless but glorious mosaics that have been waiting under the same sun for thousands of years for nothing in particular. The Mediterranean sun that reigns on high warms the tideless and capricious sea, inviting you to bob around in it without purpose until you decide with equal caprice that it's time to get out of the water. Not because you've arrived at your destination, but because the position of the sun or the hollers from the pier suggest it. Or because you caught sight of a palm tree or a pine offering some welcome shade.

People go to the North Sea to walk up and down the beach, to go for a dip or take the ferry to England. And when they've done what they came to do, they go home. The Mediterranean Sea, by contrast, is a means rather than an end, a resource for life, a way of deciding where you stand with respect to the past and the present. The only pedagogical lesson it has to teach – and no one ever put it better than Kafavis – is that we're always on the move, that perfection is not to be found in the goal of our journey, but somewhere along the way, and that it's better to enjoy as much of what life has to offer as we live it. Otherwise there's a danger that you'll realize when you reach the end that you passed perfection long ago and didn't notice. It sounds like a clash of clichés, and perhaps it is, but they're clichés 'kept for re-order', as the old-fashioned photographer's studio would have it.

The shortest summary of the gulf I've been describing is perhaps found in the Ladino saying Matvejević quotes on the last page of his book: '*Dame al mazal e etcha me a la mar*', or 'Make me happy and throw me into the sea'. For those who feel at home in Zandvoort on the North Sea, the idea of being 'thrown into the sea' will elicit thoughts of an involuntary cold bath to be resisted at all costs. But readers more inclined to the Mediterranean will happily yield to Predrag Matvejević and let him throw them into the Med. For no reason at all.

THE CLEVERINGA SCALE

Two Ways to Be a Lawyer

eiden University professor R.P. Cleveringa, who made history with a public lecture on November 26th, 1940, when he vehemently protested the sacking of his former teacher E.M. Meijers and other Jewish professors, let his conscience speak again after the war. The second occasion was in relation to an appointment rather than a dismissal, the issue was more complex, there was no public opportunity to magnify his protest, and the majority of people (as is so often the case) had other things on their minds. The second Cleveringa protest thus enjoys significantly less recognition than the first. It turned around the following.

Rudolph Pabus Cleveringa, professor of mercantile law and civil procedural law and dean of Leiden University's

Faculty of Law, who was forced to pay for his objection to the
anti-Jewish measures of the German occupier with two periods
of six months in prison, became chairman, after the liberation
in 1945, of a commission set up to purify Leiden's student community of traitors and collaborators. Students who had signed
the so-called 'student declaration', hoping, among other things,
to avoid forced labor in Germany, were informed via a radio
address delivered by the Minister of Education, Art, and Science
on August 24th, 1945, that the government was extremely serious in its plans to sweep the Dutch academic house clean. The
minister addressed them in the following words:

> *The assignees, however, will presently have to accept the conse-*
> *quences of their decision. [...] Many of those who had to decide*
> *were still very young. A great many, alas, can seek exoneration*
> *in the advice of their professors. But none of this changes the*
> *fact that they made the wrong decision. They cannot appeal to*
> *the national interest that has need of an educated generation.*
> *The nation's honor precedes its interest.*

I am not aware if Cleveringa was listening to the radio
on August 24th, 1945, but the resolute words of the recently
appointed minister – Gerardus van der Leeuw, former pastor
and professor of theology at the University of Groningen –
will not have gone down very well in whatever way he finally
heard them. After all, hadn't a significant number of the Dutch
authorities been particularly accommodating to the Germany
occupier? The permanent secretaries, the police, the civil service corps, the professors? But now the students were being

forced to take the brunt of post-war reaction with heavy-handed accusations and with 'the honor of the nation' being tossed in their faces!

BEFORE LOOKING AT WHAT CLEVERINGA DID NEXT, THE reader might be interested to know the content of the declaration every student was expected to sign in the spring of 1943:

> *The undersigned [...] hereby solemnly declares on his word of honor that he will conscientiously conform to the laws, decrees and other dispositions in force in Dutch occupied territory, and will abstain from any act directed against the German Reich or the Dutch authorities or engage in any activity that might imperil public order in the institutes of higher education in view of the present circumstances.*

Quite an alarming declaration to have your nose rubbed into, and not exactly surprising that the majority of the close to 15,000 Dutch students at the time refused to sign it. More than 2,000, however, *did* sign the declaration, among them both NSB (Dutch National Socialist Movement) sympathizers and people who were or had been active in the student resistance. Of those who refused to sign, roughly 3,500 were sent to Germany and put to work in the country's war industry.

But the student declaration of 1943 is far less ominous than the declaration that was presented for signature in 1940 – a full two and a half years earlier – to every Dutch government official. It was that declaration, the so-called Aryan Declaration, that directly occasioned the dismissal of a number of Leiden professors and thus also the Cleveringa protest of November 26th, 1940. Here too it is useful to familiarize ourselves with the exact content of the declaration that officials were expected to sign:

> *The undersigned [...] declares according to the best of his/her knowledge that neither he/she him/herself, nor his/her partner/ fiancé/ée, nor one of his/her/their parents or grandparents has ever belonged to the Jewish faith community.*
>
> *The undersigned is aware that he/she exposes him/herself to immediate dismissal should the preceding declaration prove to be incorrect.*

Every civil servant in the Netherlands received two variants of this declaration on October 5th, 1940 and each was expected to fill in and sign one of the two: declaration A, which stated that they were not Jewish and thus Aryan, or declaration B, which stated that they were Jewish. One of the declarations had to be signed and submitted within three weeks; otherwise the person in question was to be considered Jewish. A few weeks after the deadline, thousands of people were dismissed from their public service jobs on the basis of the completed declarations. Cleveringa was also among those to receive such an Aryan declaration in the fall of 1940, first as a deputy judge in The Hague and then as university professor alongside seventy-two of his Leiden colleagues.

Together with fellow professor Benjamin Telders, Cleveringa tried his utmost to persuade if not all then at least a considerable number of the members of Leiden's professorial corps not to sign, but his efforts were to no avail. All of them signed. The best they were able to achieve for their endeavors was to have sixty Leiden professors include a letter of protest drawn up by Telders when they submitted their completed Aryan Declaration.

The situation wasn't much different in other departments of the machinery of government. The permanent secretaries, the commissioners of police, the provincial and local civil servants, and even the Supreme Court justices signed the declaration and later stood idly by when Mr Lodewijk Ernst Visser, president of the Netherlands' highest court of justice, was dismissed from his post by the German occupying authorities on November 21st, 1940 for no other reason than the fact of his Jewish origins.

SO IT'S EASY TO IMAGINE WHY CLEVERINGA WAS STILL troubled to some degree by the entire student cleansing policy in the months that followed liberation. Students who had been obliged in 1943 to declare that they would not imperil the public order at the university were now being threatened with suspension, i.e. exclusion from classes and exams for varying periods of time. The majority of civil servants, judges, and police officials, on the other hand, were simply left to continue their work or resume it, in spite of the fact that they had first facilitated the identification of their Jewish compatriots, then their disenfranchisement and ultimate persecution by signing the Aryan Declaration *en masse* three years earlier.

The last straw for Cleveringa was the recommendation submitted to the House of Representatives on December 13th,

1945, concerning a number of vacant seats on the Supreme Court. The name P.H. Smits figured on the recommendation, a man who had served as a member of the country's highest court since 1941 and throughout the remainder of the occupation. While Smits' judicial talents were never called into question – he had already been recommended for a vacancy in the 1930s – the very fact that he had been appointed by the Nazi *Reichskommissar to the Netherlands* Arthur Seyss-Inquart was reason enough to make him a controversial magistrate. As court justice during the occupation, moreover, he shared responsibility for a number of questionable and plainly reprehensible judgments rendered by the Supreme Court at the time. It should have been clear to everyone that his reappointment would only serve to further undermine the Supreme Court's already sullied reputation. The House of Representatives was clearly not wholehearted in approving Smits' appointment. Three ballots were required, and in the last analysis the appointment was only agreed on the basis of a rather slim majority, 35 votes to 31. Cleveringa was unable to swallow Smits' reappointment and resigned in protest as chair of Leiden's Student Purification Committee.

RUDOLPH PABUS CLEVERINGA EVIDENTLY HAD A built-in moral compass, a conscience so aligned that he was not inclined to hesitation, where others, based on a multitude of considerations and excuses, demonstrated their capacity to accommodate when faced with emerging injustice or injustice that was already burgeoning. In a book review published a few years later in *De Gids* – the Netherlands' oldest literary journal – he further underlined his critical stance towards the practice of law during the German occupation, which resulted in an angry letter to the editor from someone connected to the District Court in The Hague. The keenness of his capacity to judge is always in evidence together with the purity with which he deployed his sense of justice. In a time like ours, when some historians consider it fashionable to pretend that it's impossible to make a distinction between right and wrong, as if morality is nothing more than an opinion with hindsight, it comes as a genuine pleasure to see the needle of Cleveringa's compass pointing resolutely in the direction of justice, in spite of the solemn and outmoded legal language in which his ideas are expressed.

One might be inclined to wonder where Cleveringa picked up his sense of moral direction. What gave this reputable and meticulous jurist such certainty in the face of historical danger and human injustice, while many other equally reputable and meticulous jurists (and non-jurists) were of the opinion that it was better, all things considered and 'to prevent worse', to stay in their jobs and try to make a difference in silence while continuing to support their families? What constitutes the 'Cleveringa factor', the factor that transformed this circumspect expert in mercantile and maritime law, to quote Kees Schuyt, into 'an icon of intellectual resistance against oppression and inhumanity'?

There probably is a biographical or historical answer to these questions, although such would demand detailed research. A psychologizing answer might also be possible, although it would remain speculative by its very nature. To my mind, however, it would be more in the spirit of Cleveringa to suppose that this 'Cleveringa factor' is present in everyone, at least in theory. After all, wasn't everyone convinced to a greater or lesser degree that the decision of the anti-Semitic Nazi regime occupying the Netherlands to employ official forms to identify Jewish civil servants was only the beginning of something much, much worse? Everyone must surely have realized how unfair it was to treat students, who had signed a promise in their late teens or early twenties that they would behave themselves towards the authorities, as if they were traitors and collaborators. And wasn't it painfully obvious to every Dutch jurist worth his or her salt that the reappointment of a senior justice who had spent four years of the occupation 'accommodating' the Germans was a slap in the face of the victims of persecution, the men and women of the resistance and other 'loyal patriots'? In short, it's not so much a question of our capacity to distinguish between right and wrong, it's more about what we actually do when confronted with this difference.

PERHAPS THE BEST WAY TO ILLUSTRATE THE 'Cleveringa-factor' is to present it in contrast to another figure representing the opposite end of the spectrum, someone we might identify in this regard as an anti-Cleveringa; a brilliant jurist who travelled a diametrically conflicting path, namely that of evil, of amorality, of totalitarian opportunism; a jurist who was the same age as Cleveringa – they were born only five months apart – and whose illustrious legal career in Germany was equal to that of Cleveringa in the Netherlands; a man whose prominence on the black pages of twentieth century legal history is just as conspicuous as Cleveringa's on the white.

His name is Roland Freisler. After taking his finals at the Wilhelmsgymnasium in Kassel in 1912, he turned his scholarly attention to the study of law at the University of Jena, which he interrupted in 1914 to serve his fatherland and volunteer for military service. He was taken prisoner by the Russians on the Eastern Front in 1915, and it is probable that he returned to Germany only in 1920. He defended his dissertation in Jena two years later – on the foundational principles of industrial organization – and graduated as a Doctor of Law. He set himself up in legal practice, and via his defense of a number of NSDAP members (*Nationalsozialistische Deutsche Arbeiterpartei* – known in English as the Nazi Party) he became involved with and joined the party in 1923.

In addition to his legal practice, Freisler was politically active from 1925 onwards, first as city councilor in Kassel, later as a member of the Prussian *Landtag* (State Parliament). Senior civil service appointments at the Prussian Ministry of Justice paved the way for his promotion to Secretary of State in the *Reichsministerium für Justiz* after the Nazis seized power in 1933. In this position, he participated in the infamous Wannsee Conference in January 1942. As head of the criminal law department of the Academy for German Law, moreover, he also contributed to the formulation and development of a penal code adapted to the Nazi social order. In that system – and I limit myself here to simple and constitutional terms – the interests of the German nation transcended those of the individual. The will of the German people was embodied in the country's leader, thus focusing absolute legislative, executive and judiciary power in a single person.

ONE CONSEQUENCE OF THE NATIONAL SOCIALIST vision of society and law was the existence of the so-called *Volksgerichtshof* or People's Court in Berlin. The *Volksgerichtshof* was first established by Adolf Hitler in 1934 out of dissatisfaction over the outcome of the Reichstag Fire case. Two years later, the court's jurisdiction was extended from instances of treason and high treason to the adjudication of political crimes in general, activities, in other words, that the Nazi regime considered undesirable. Of this *Volksgerichtshof* Dr. Roland Freisler became president on August 20th, 1942.

The *Volksgerichtshof* consisted of a number of chambers (referred to as 'senates'), each of which consisted in its turn of two professional judges appointed by Hitler and three lay justices. It goes without saying that the latter were always faithful party functionaries. Suspects were not allowed to choose their own lawyer, legal proceedings were conducted and settled at a furious tempo, and Freisler himself devoted much of his energy during court sittings to intimidating suspects as much as he could and disconcerting them. The thousands of people condemned to death by the *Volksgerichtshof* during the years of the war included men and women who were active in anti-Nazi resistance, such as the members of the *Die Weisse Rose* or The White Rose, the *Rote Kapelle* or the Red Orchestra and the *Kreisauer Kreis* or Kreisau Circle. The conspirators responsible for the failed attempt on Adolf Hitler's life on July 20th, 1944 were also tried by Roland Freisler's *Volksgerichtshof*. A number of recordings of the interrogations can be found on YouTube, filmed in the courtroom itself on Hitler's orders. The restructuring of the administration of justice to accommodate political terror went so far that not only those who committed or contemplated armed resistance were brought before the *Volksgerichtshof*. In addition to treason, deeds and statements that were considered 'a threat to the defensibility of the German nation' were sufficient to occasion a summons.

One example from among very many relates to the gifted Dutch pianist Karlrobert Kreiten, who had studied under Claudio Arrau, among others, and performed with success under the baton of Wilhelm Furtwängler. During a concert series in Berlin in 1943, Kreiten stayed with a childhood girlfriend of his German mother. During dinner, however, he made a few negative remarks about Adolf Hitler, describing him as shameless, sick, deranged. The lady of the house considered it her National Socialist duty to ask the advice of a couple of friends as to whether she should take the matter further. The ladies thought she should, and as a result an official complaint was lodged that led to Kreiten's arrest on May 3rd, 1943, the eve of a concert he was scheduled to give in Heidelberg. He was held in custody for four months and then sentenced by the First Senate of the *Volksgerichtshof*, under the chairmanship of its president, Roland Freisler. The court condemned him to death. Appeals for clemency, petitions, and even a personal intervention on the part of Wilhelm Furtwängler, were to no avail. Kreiten was executed on September 7th in Berlin's Plötzensee prison, one of the thousands of victims of a perverted legal system appropriately styled *Terrorjustiz* or justice by exercising terror.

Roland Freisler was the personification *par excellence* of such German *Terrorjustiz*. He was fanatical, prejudiced, and inclined to indulge in long humiliating tirades against the suspects who appeared before him. The shrieking voice that carried his tirades earned him the nickname 'raging Roland', and the technicians charged with recording court proceedings had a hard time regulating the volume in such a way that he could be understood. He did not permit suspects to appear in court clean shaven and even insisted on occasion that their belts and suspenders be confiscated, leaving them scruffy looking and down at heel. He thus ranted against retired army general Erwin von Witzleben – one of the men involved in the attempted assassination of Hitler on July 20th, 1944: 'You dirty old man. Why are you constantly fiddling with your pants?'

RUDOLPH PABUS CLEVERINGA AND ROLAND FREISLER. It's almost painful to reference both names in a single sentence. While they may have been contemporaries, their lives were poles apart. Nevertheless, they were both eminent jurists, and both, by coincidence, specialists in mercantile law and procedural law. One worked as a company lawyer, the other as an attorney; both were judges and both were professors of law. If Freisler symbolizes absolute zero on the justice scales then Cleveringa must surely represent the highest point thereof. Confronted by such extremes, one is inclined to wonder whether it is even possible to include both these jurists under a single system of morality.

Perhaps inspiration can be sought from the way the Swede Anders Celsius arrived at his calibration of the thermometer. He took the melting temperature of ice and the boiling point of water and he divided the difference between both temperatures into a hundred degrees. As a result, we all know what we mean when we say it's 18° Celsius outside. In a similar manner we could divide, by way of a thought experiment, the distance between Freisler's absolute zero and Cleveringa's highest point into one hundred degrees, thus providing ourselves with an instrument or scale to measure the moral demeanor of jurists.

Let's put the 'Cleveringa Scale' to the test. When Fred Teeven, State Secretary for Justice in the present Dutch legislature, declared that the killing of a burglar by a resident may be unfortunate, but that it is 'one of the risks' burglars are taking, where on our scale would we be inclined to locate a jurist who makes such statements? And what should we think of Amsterdam lawyer Bram Moszkowicz, who claimed that he was under no obligation to adopt the professional standards expected of lawyers? Or of Dutch Minister of Justice Ivo Opstelten who launched a plan to give the government the authority to tap into private computers? The same minister Opstelten who posed in full regalia for an official photo with all the presidents of *his* tribunals and courts of justice, while Montesquieu's *trias politica* principle states with sufficient clarity that they are not *his* tribunals or courts of justice? What would these lawyers score on the Cleveringa scale? 83? 76? 98?

IF CLEVERINGA'S EXEMPLARY ATTITUDE DURING AND after the war has anything to teach us – certainly when offset against the ink-black counter image of Roland Freisler – then it has to be that only one thing matters when the hour of truth comes: it's not about what you say you're going to do, nor what you'll say afterwards in hindsight, but what you actually do at the moment it has to be done. Such decisive action at the right moment is referred to in German by the handsome term *Zivilcourage*, a word roughly equivalent to the English 'courage of one's conviction'. The hypothetical Dutch equivalent *burgermoed* doesn't appear in recent editions of the standard Dutch lexica. The German term might best be translated 'heroic courage in plain clothes', or in other words, acting with heroic courage without a uniform.

Heroic courage is difficult to assess when we associate it with soldiers and civilians; and the same is true for professors in gowns and judges in court regalia. Intangible powers and phenomena need a scale against which we can evaluate their efficacy, to be able to inform one another – also across generations – how dire or how innocent it was. Earthquakes are measured according to the Richter Scale, allowing us to compare the Lisbon earthquake of 1755 with the San Francisco earthquake of 1906. Wind-force is measured on the Beaufort Scale, an instrument that likewise facilitates universal comparisons. The Cleveringa Scale should allow us henceforth to assess the moral character, ethical vigor, and sense of justice of those engaged in the legal profession.

Such rankings, of course, are far from easy to apply. A great deal of heated discussion is likely to accompany any attempt to determine a lawyer's place on the Cleveringa Scale: should it be 78 or 53 or 91? But I am personally inclined to consider debates of this sort as something to look forward to. European Commissioner for Justice Viviane Reding has recently moved in a similar direction with her call for a 'justice index' applicable in every member state. While earthquakes and storm winds are brute and inarticulate forces of nature, the true beauty of a Cleveringa Scale might be that it could allow us, on the basis of such a ranking, not only to assess others, but in particular also to assess ourselves; jurists or not.

HAMLET AND TELEMACHUS

Two Sons

Telemachus and Hamlet. Both unmarried and, on the surface at least, ideal sons-in-law. Both are saddled with the task of avenging their father and restoring his honor. Both long for sufficient courage to grow within them so that they can do what a ghostly apparition asks from them. Both brood at the spectacle of their mother; her reputation is on the line since their father disappeared. Both are notorious doubters, partly because of their character, partly because of their still youthful age. Both – each according to the literary rhetoric of his day – find themselves at the beginning of the story in a contemplative and dispirited mood on account of the loss of their father, a mood that doesn't inspire the decisive intervention to which they are challenged by the apparition.

'Who has ever really known who gave him life?' Telemachus sighs. 'Would to god I'd been the son of a happy man whom old age overtook in the midst of his possessions!' Hamlet laments that even 'bounded in a nutshell' he could count himself a 'king of infinite space', were it not for his bad dreams. Both thus torment themselves with their futile ponderings, close to collapse under the burden of fate's charge, under the crushing example of their father, who surpassed everyone in power and courage.

As the ghostly manifestation puts it to the elder of the two sons: 'Few sons are the equal of their fathers; most fall short, all too few surpass them.'

TELEMACHUS AT ELSINORE; HAMLET ON ITHACA. Picture the castle of the spinelessly murdered Danish king in an amusing thought experiment as the decor for Penelope and her suitors, and – vice versa – the court of Claudius and Gertrude flown over as it were to the Ionian Islands. The only one who would survive in one piece would probably be Laertes, the brother of Hamlet's ill-fated love Ophelia, who would reencounter himself on the distant Greek island as the similarly named elderly father of Odysseus.

In the third scene of the first act of Hamlet, this same Laertes declares of Hamlet, his brother-in-law to be: 'His will is not his own. / For he himself is subject to his birth.' In a brief couplet we are presented with the thematic problem that is to torment both Hamlet and Telemachus their entire literary lives: what to do; how to do justice to one's calling in life and to the example of an incomparable father; how to acquire knowledge of what divine fate has prescribed?

THERE'S DOUBTLESS MUCH TO BE SAID AGAINST A COMparison between Homer's creation and that of Shakespeare, but from what we have said thus far we can observe at the very least that Telemachus and Hamlet are kindred literary sons. Both are overshadowed by their great mythical example Orestes. He, Orestes, at least knew what to do, and Aeschylus' *Oresteia* would be far from misplaced as a set of course notes for the undecided. Indeed, Orestes took merciless revenge on Aegisthus, the cunning killer of his father Agamemnon, slain on his return from the Trojan war.

Telemachus is already presented with the bold Orestes by way of example in the first book of the *Odyssey*, and by none less than the goddess Athena. 'Be as brave,' she tells Telemachus, appearing to him in the form of the stranger Mentor, a Taphian prince. Still lacking in purpose, the young son of Odysseus, who can only stand and watch as boisterous suitors compete with ever diminishing shame for the hand of his mother, receives even more useful advice from Athena. Setting herself up as the protector of both father and son, the goddess urges Telemachus to go on a journey – a mini-*Odyssey* if you like – to Pylos and Sparta, the respective kingdoms of Nestor and Menelaus. He is to inquire of both kings – his father's erstwhile companions-in-arms – whether Odysseus is still alive and on his way back from Ithaca. Whatever their response, the goddess insists that he must finally do something: 'Take matters into your own hands," Athena urges, offering him the choice between deception and open combat. Hamlet could have used such a goddess, someone who would have urged him to act in such an efficacious manner. Instead,

Hamlet racks his brains with a theoretical dilemma: whether it be nobler to suffer or take arms against a sea of troubles.

IN 'SANDY PYLOS', IN NESTOR'S PALACE, TELEMACHUS is hammered once again with the inspiring example of Orestes. 'See what a good thing it is,' says the venerable king, 'for a man to leave a son behind him to do as Orestes did, who killed false Aegisthus the murderer of his noble father. You too, then – for I see you are tall and handsome – must show your mettle and make yourself a name; then later generations will sing your praises.'

The young Telemachus responds with the following answer, so characteristic of his vacillating temperament and youthful diffidence: 'Would that the gods might grant me the strength to exact like vengeance on the wicked suitors for their woeful misdeeds and reckless overconfidence. But the gods have no such happiness in store for me nor for my father, so I am doomed to bear it as best I can."

IN SPARTA, WHILE STAYING WITH MENELAUS AND Helena, Telemachus has a more purposeful and decisive air about him. It is here, in the fourth book of the *Odyssey*, that the exhortations and inspiration of Athena begin to have a tangible effect.

In books 5 to 14 of the twenty-four book epic, Telemachus does not play a visibly significant role. It is Odysseus' own per-egrinations the reader now hears about, which he recounts on being asked at the court of the king and queen of the *Phaeacians*. But in the meantime, in reality a matter of a mere few weeks,

Telemachus has evolved from an indecisive boy into an intelligent and dynamic young man. He rejects an invitation to remain in Sparta longer than is necessary. As soon as he hears from Menelaus about his father's wanderings and his involuntary stay on the island of Ogygia, detained by the nymph Calypso, he takes his leave, politely but firmly. The pressure exerted on him by the king of Sparta to stay twelve more days, and the impatience of Telemachus who experiences his call to act more urgently than before, together form a delicate counterpoint to the imprisonment his father Odysseus was forced to endure for many years on his journey home.

Menelaus likewise does not fail to mention the courageous and persevering Orestes, the avenger of his brother Agamemnon. After Athena and Nestor, Telemachus is here confronted with this explicit example for the third time in short succession.

IN THE MEANTIME ODYSSEUS ARRIVES ON ITHACA, transformed beyond recognition into an old beggar by the goddess Athena. When Telemachus returns unscathed to the island by ship shortly thereafter, the familiar denouement unavoidably unfolds, restoring Odysseus to his throne and to Penelope's marital bed, while each of her suitors tastes defeat. Only the singer and collaborator Phemius is spared, having argued that he was forced to perform for Penelope's suitors against his will.

Observe, however, what has happed to the young Telemachus in this relatively short period of time. After his minor odyssey in the Peloponnese and his conversations with Nestor and Menelaus, and inspired above all by the guidance of Athena, the youthful character has undergone a critical evolution. He is now more energetic, even more brazen and defiant in face of his mother's suitors. He expresses himself with greater clarity and his presence is more robust, so much so that even Penelope concludes on his return from Sparta that at least her son no longer offers a reason for her prolonged life of widowhood. Telemachus thus functions in the story once again as a catalyst in the contest for her hand organized by Penelope among the suitors, which is won by Odysseus with flying colors. Telemachus then fights at his father's side to secure the reputation of palace and queen, and his own reputation as his father's son.

Time to bring in the arch-doubter Hamlet. 'My thoughts be bloody, or be nothing worth!' he says, spurring himself on to no avail in one of his renowned soliloquies. Hamlet remains in his bloody thoughts and becomes thereby an example of existential indecision and inertia for countless dramatic and novelistic heroes after him. Telemachus, on the other hand, manages to transform his bloody thoughts into long-anticipated deeds. In the Odyssey's forty-one day time span, courage does indeed swell up within him. The son of Odysseus grows, perhaps even surpassing himself, from someone who believed he was 'doomed to be patient' into someone who knows how to win over the gods and keep them on his side, who knows how to act effectively and succeed with honors in fulfilling the supreme task to which he is predestined in the story of his life.

WITH RESPECT TO TELEMACHUS, THE ODYSSEY MIGHT be described – with a little good will – as a proto-*Bildungsroman* or coming-of-age novel, and Odysseus' son as the young hero of this literary manifestation. Telemachus may even be the first fictional character in western literature to experience genuine personality development within a single book. Thus seen, he is clearly the more modern of the two sons juxtaposed here and thereby the most timeless. As such, he haunts the pages of many later novels and plays about sons and fathers, even Shakespeare's tragedy about the ever-indecisive Danish prince. Instead of wandering lost over Ithaca's rocky inclines, Telemachus paces back and forth – like an older brother, an ancient shadow – at Hamlet's side on the misty battlements of Elsinore. Hamlet himself, who had the gift of words but not of deeds, would say: 'The counterfeit presentment of two brothers.'

THE QUESTIONABLE PROBLEM

On the Logic of Suicide

urope, Italy, Turin – behold the Dantesque circles within which the fragile and congenial chemist-writer Primo Levi managed to live and move in the most admirable way for more than forty years after his incredible experiences in Auschwitz. The central point of these circles is the apartment building on the Corso Re Umberto, the home in which he was born in 1919 and where in 1987 he also met his end. His work is the unsurpassed account of his unimaginable experiences. If there was ever an example of a writer who had no need of a biography it was Primo Levi. Introductions to his life and work, collections of interviews, have circulated for years in every shape and form and constitute, on occasion, an interesting explanation of his work or serve to supplement it. But everything Primo Levi had to offer the outside world can be found in his work itself: in testimonies, novels, stories, essays, poems, columns, and a personal anthology of the work of authors who formed him. He wrote about his own life in such a clear and penetrating manner that no biographer can gain much credit from the task. There is only one part of his life about which he did not write and that is the way in which it came to an end. And it is precisely this event that seems to have such a unique capacity to attract biographers and other interpreters.

The concrete circumstances under which Levi passed away are plain and simple. On April 11th, 1987 around 10 in the morning, Primo Levi opened the door of his third floor apartment to Jolanda Gasperi, the female concierge of the building in which he lived. Gasperi handed him his mail as she did every day and didn't notice anything out of the ordinary. Levi thanked her in the friendly manner to which she had grown accustomed and she made her way back downstairs. A few minutes later she heard a dull thud in the stairwell. She peered through the window of her concierge's office and hurried outside. She found the already lifeless body of dottore Levi on the stone floor behind the elevator, bleeding from the head.

Countless journalists, commentators, and writers, as well as the author of the first substantial biography of Levi, have swallowed one single interpretation of these events hook, line, and sinker: Primo Levi committed suicide. It has to be admitted that many survivors of the German camps – among them a number of distinguished writers – have taken their own life, and some at an advanced age. And Levi had indeed spoken about suicide in several places in his work. Add to this his failing health and troublesome domestic situation, sharing a home with a ninety-one year old mother suffering from dementia. But I have never seen the question posed with clarity and sufficient weight in the extensive literature surrounding Primo Levi: can we 'thus' conclude that Levi committed suicide?

Myriam Anissimov, the author of the first major biography of Primo Levi entitled *Primo Levi ou la tragédie d'un optimiste – Primo Levi. Tragedy of an Optimist,* has no scruples whatsoever on the matter. From the first to the last page of her book – and there are no fewer than 698 of them in the original French edition – she presumes suicide axiomatically. Indeed, she continuously uses suicide in her approach to Levi's entire life, thereby making it appear hopeless and desperate. On the very first page of her introduction she states: 'This gentle, reserved and unassuming man [...] chose a violent and dramatic death.' And on the following page she informs the reader: 'A storm of sudden violence tore through the careful reserve of Primo Levi on the morning he went out to the landing and threw himself down from the third floor.' One passage in the biography takes the cake when it comes to the blind and uncritical way Anissimov takes her point of departure – namely suicide – to be incontrovertible. She writes on page 6: 'He left no message, so it would be mere speculation to list the possible reasons he may have had for choosing death, and that particular death.'

One could call it 'mere speculation', but as a biographer it might be better to ask oneself aloud whether it would not have been more logical for the writer Primo Levi – presuming he did indeed plan to commit suicide – to have left some kind of note for his wife, mother, and children. One might also, and perhaps should also, ask oneself – but Myriam Anissimov fails to do so – whether it would not have made more sense for Primo Levi the chemist to have chosen a less risky way out, such as a chemical concoction or an overdose of medication. A three story fall has every chance of leading to permanent invalidity or serious brain damage rather than death. And contra every quotation from Levi's work, correspondence, and published interviews in which he alludes to the possibility and the problem of suicide, a plethora of similar statements can be found in which he makes it clear that he has already left suicide behind him as it were, that he has dealt with it. The one-sided suggestive quotations Myriam Anissimov uses to pepper the pages of her book do not even begin to function as evidence in support of the suicide she takes as read, just as the more cheerful and positive quotations that might be set against such a presupposition are unable to prove the contrary. Acquiescing to the latter would result in a mock battle – both pointless and speculative in equal measure – with contradictory and tendentious quotations.

Towards the end of her book, Myriam Anissimov makes brief reference to the fact that Rita Levi-Montalcini and David Mendel, two people who were exceptionally close to Primo Levi, each in their own way, have always refused to believe that his death was suicide. But the biographer does not make the effort to explore such authoritative opinions or the counterevidence, while Nobel Prize winner Rita Levi-Montalcini, for example, who had been the writer's friend for forty years, already declared in a comprehensive interview in the Italian weekly *Panorama* on May 3rd, 1987: 'Primo Levi era assolutamente contrario al suicidio.'

After a terrifying year in the hell of a concentration camp, Primo Levi had every reason in the world to commit suicide. But this is an isolated circumstance that cannot simply be used as implicit evidence in support of the claim that he actually did. Who among us would dare to maintain that suicide is the result of a logical process? That a sufficiently valid reason to commit suicide must 'thus' lead to suicide? And which reason is valid enough to justify suicide from the perspective of logic or at least be its logical cause?

That question can only be answered in theory, as an outsider, since at first sight the would-be suicide who has decided to hasten his or her hour, is no longer likely to have a clear picture of his reasons. Or perhaps the picture is all too clear. Even an apparently minor reason can come so close that it fills a person's entire mental horizon, so much so that the so-called 'homo suicidalis' can no longer see beyond it. I was once told the story of an inventor working for the Swedish firm SSA Socker who devised a revolutionary folded and glue-free wrapper for two sugar cubes, allowing the user to retrieve both cubes with a simple movement of the fingers without having to tear the wrapper. As long as you know, of course, how to deploy the simple finger movement. If you don't know, you're doomed to fiddle and fumble to no avail. The consumer ultimately judged this ingenious discovery so illogical that the product was a complete failure and a humiliating commercial flop for the manufacturer. The inventor was so overwhelmed by the embarrassment that he committed suicide.

It's hard to find words to support the idea of someone ending their life in shame for the sake of a couple of sugar cubes.

But it would appear in practice that every reason for suicide is potentially valid enough, thus raising the question whether it makes sense to be talking about 'reasons' in the first place. Perhaps it's just a quirk of fate that determines the moment at which one opts to do the very thing for which every reason pales into insignificance, even reasons that appear at first sight to be incredibly logical.

The question we should be asking about the death of Primo Levi is thus not whether he intended to commit suicide, not whether he had sufficient 'reason' to do so; the only question is: did he or didn't he? And in the absence of an unambiguous answer supported by the facts, extreme reticence and extreme respect are the only appropriate response. No less respect than is due to the memory of those who patently *did* take their own lives.

Primo Levi's open-ended demise ought likewise to be approached with the same caution, because the enigma of his death can be considered emblematic in a certain sense of philosophical reflection on suicide. Albert Camus may well have said that suicide is the only interesting philosophical problem, but as is often the case with philosophical problems: 'the proof of the pudding' is ultimately 'in the eating'. And most people – philosophers or not – who are preoccupied with the problem of suicide might talk about the pudding, exchange correspondence on it and write about it, but in the last analysis they don't eat it.

'I MAY KILL MYSELF, / BUT I CANNOT DIE'. THESE WORDS were written by the Japanese poet Oka Masafumi shortly before he jumped to his death from a tall building on July 17th, 1975.

I don't precisely know who Oka Masafumi was and these two lines are all I've read of his work; but there's one other thing I know about him: he was twelve years old when he died.

Such youthful suicides are far from unique in Japan, which was known as 'the land of suicide' even before the publication of Émile Durkheim's renowned study *Sur le suicide*, the first standard work on the subject. If it is true that a phenomenon acquires increasing prominence in a given culture the more names the said culture evolves for it – 'sea' among the Greeks and 'snow' among the Inuit – then suicide must indeed be considered a characteristic feature of Japanese culture. Based on a cursory study I managed to uncover the following list of Japanese terms, all of which designate one or other variant of suicide: harakiri and seppuku – concepts everyone knows – but also ikka shinjū, jibaku, jisatsu, junshi, kaizubara, kanshi, munenbara, oibara, oyaku shinjū, shinjū, sokotsushi and tsumebara, bringing the provisional total to fourteen. 'Sokotsushi', for example, is suicide rooted in remorse on account of inadvertence, because one wrongly failed to notice something. 'Tsumebara' is the obligatory suicide of the samurai who has been condemned to death, and 'shinjū' designates the double suicide of lovers, while 'ikka shinjū' is family suicide, usually that of the mother who first kills her own child(ren) then herself. Suicide in Japan has been an artistically refined social grace for centuries.

If such subtle variants exist between the different forms of suicide, then it's all the more important to ensure that those one leaves behind understand the precise reasons why one has chosen to die. In Japan, the farewell letter of the person taking his or her leave, often in the form of or accompanied by a poem, can almost be described as a literary genre in itself. It is not without reason that the international chapter 'Around the World' of Marc Etkind's *Or Not to Be. A Collection of Suicide Notes* begins with an overview of Japanese suicide notes.

A uniquely laden example of this Japanese tradition of suicide letter writing is to be found in relation to the military suicide squads who endeavored to destroy American marine vessels at sea or from the air during the final months of the Second World War (between October 1944 and August 1945). Made up of young men between the ages of twenty and twenty five, the suicide squads had their immediate origin in a variety of spontaneous actions, such as that of seventeen pilots who carried out a suicidal air attack on an American marine flotilla on June 20th, 1944. The attack was a failure, and only five of the seventeen returned alive to their Iwojima base. But their initiative had a more than inspiring effect on the Japanese troops who found themselves at that moment in hopelessly dire straits, and it didn't take long for their action to be systematized.

In October 1944, vice-admiral Ōnishi Takijirō (1891-1945), commander of the Japanese air fleet on the Philippines and one of the 'spiritual fathers' of the attack on Pearl Harbor in 1941, gave a speech to his officers at the military camp in Mabalacat. He appealed to them to make the ultimate patriotic sacrifice, jibaku, i.e. attack by 'self-explosion'. No one objected – so the tradition would have us believe – and the idea was immediately implemented. In the months that followed, thousands of young soldiers came forward for the so-called

Tokkōtai, a word composed of three syllables from the full name Shimpū Tokubetsu Kōkegitai, or 'Special Attack Forces of the Divine Wind'. In the west they were better known as the 'kamikaze' ('Divine wind'), the Japanese equivalent for the Sino-Japanese Shimpū.

Most kamikaze flights were made in ordinary planes; the specially designed steerable flying bombs named Ōka – Japanese for cherry blossom – were a later development. A total of 4615 Japanese young men met their death in this manner, in contrast to a total of 34 sunk and 288 damaged American ships. Each pilot – successful or not – was posthumously promoted in rank and treated as a 'living god' for the fulfillment of his patriotic duty in the service of the Japanese empire.

The fact that many of these suicide pilots left a legacy to the world in the form of letters, diary entries and poems has everything to do with the military procedure whereby they were informed, mostly one day before, of their 'honorable' selection for a mission. From that moment until the moment they climbed aboard their flying coffins after a farewell ceremony at long tables set with bottles of cold sake, they had the opportunity to come to terms with their life and impending death. The messages they left behind often included locks of hair and nail clippings, something to be buried after they were gone. Collections of their farewell letters appeared in Japan after the war under florid titles such as *To Distant Mountain Streams* and *Hear the Voices of the Ocean*.

The final letter of kamikaze pilot Matsuo Isao is a typical example, containing a variety of fixed elements from the genre of the Japanese military suicide note:

Dear Parents,

Please congratulate me. I have been granted a magnificent
opportunity to die. This is my last day. The fate of our father-
land depends on the battle at sea south of here, in which I shall
fall like the blossom of a splendid cherry tree. [...]

    To be able to die as a man is an opportunity I know how
to appreciate. From the bottom of my heart I am grateful to the
parents who raised me with their unremitting prayers and their
tender love. And I am equally thankful for the way in which
my squadron commander and the senior officers have taken care
of me as if I was their own son and for the meticulous training
they have given me.

    Accept my thanks, dear parents, for the twenty three years
in which you cared for me and inspired me. I hope that the deed
I am about to perform will serve in one way or another, how-
ever small, as compensation for what you have done for me. [...]

    May our death be as sudden and pure as the shattering
of crystal.

MANY HUNDREDS OF SIMILAR LETTERS HAVE BEEN
passed down to us, most with haiku and tanka as poetic addi-
tions, one even more grandiloquent than another. Perhaps the
most heartrending farewell message of them all, however, is that
of vice-admiral Ōnishi himself, the man who devised the ghastly
kamikaze technique in the first place. On August 15th, 1945,
after the atom bombs dropped on Nagasaki and Hiroshima
had forced Japan to capitulate, the 54-year-old military leader
retired to his office, knelt on the floor and cut open his belly
crossways (in line with seppuku ritual) using a borrowed sword.

But the weapon turned out not to be sharp enough and he suffered hours of pain-racked consciousness before death finally delivered him. In addition to his last will and testament and a farewell haiku for his wife, we also have an emotional farewell letter addressed to the spirits of 'his' deceased kamikaze pilots:

> *I want to express by deepest appreciation for the spirits of those courageous special attackers* [military euphemism for suicide squadrons, MA]. *They fought and died heroically with confidence in our final victory. In death I desire to do penance for my part in the fact that the said victory was not achieved and I confess my regret to the spirits of these dead aviators and the families they left behind.*
>
> *I would like young people in Japan to see a moral in my death. [...]*
>
> *You are our nation's most precious treasure. Strive with all the passion of the special attackers for a prosperous Japan and peace on earth!*

Ōnishi's letter is both hypocritical and impertinent in equal measure, in his misplaced appeal to the youth of Japan and his overestimation of the importance of his own death. What he did, nevertheless, was completely consistent with the circumstances in which his suicide took place. In this sense, Ōnishi's deed is an example of an unambiguous and 'logical' suicide, suicide as the unavoidable conclusion to a person's life, suicide as the result of a perfect syllogism. In a certain sense, Ōnishi's suicide might even be declared 'satisfying', given that he identified himself completely with the fate of 'his' pilots in his farewell letter and in his death. To the life he had chosen to live he attached the most far-reaching and likewise self-determined consequence.

Vice-admiral Ōnishi Takijirō's funeral ceremony was a mess. In the general chaos of the capitulation, for example, insufficient wood had been provided for an appropriate coffin. The coffin in which Ōnishi's body was finally transported by truck to the crematorium was six inches too short. But the procession acquired unexpected allure when a lonely airplane from Atsugi air base suddenly appeared in the sky. It was a fighter plane belonging to the Japanese navy with a kamikaze pilot on board. It circled a few times above the funeral cortège, dipped its wings in a farewell salute and disappeared out of sight.

PRIMO LEVI AND ŌNISHI TAKIJIRŌ. FOR THE FORMER suicide was a right, for the latter an obligation, or so it would seem at first sight. But we shouldn't stop at first sight. Because there are also concentration camp survivors who claimed that they had no right to be alive, that others had been murdered in their stead and that they – the delivered – thus had a duty, an obligation to choose death. And given the complete collapse of Japanese society, vice-admiral Ōnishi could have chosen to forego suicide and save his self-justification for his trial.

Perhaps we should put it like this: Primo Levi had a right, a right thrust upon him, but there is nothing to say that he made use of it. In his own eyes and the eyes of his fellow countrymen, on the other hand, Ōnishi Takijirō had a personal moral obligation, the moral rationale of which might be open to question.

In his self-chosen death, Ōnishi confronts us with a suicide that for westerners at least has the features of a work of art. Ritual form and moral content, complete with farewell poetry and a letter for future generations, combine to construct a composition that, in spite of its curious aesthetic appeal, might also be styled 'entartet' or 'degenerate'. Did the death of Primo Levi, understood as an 'inescapable' suicide, have the same dire appeal for someone like Myriam Anissimov? In all probability.

'Do not fall in love with questionable problems,' Levi advised his readers in 'Hatching the Cobra', one of his last essays. He was alluding to nuclear armament and other morally laden, technical discoveries, but his warning applies equally to suicide.

NAPOLEON AND ME
IN ALKMAAR

A Shared Footnote

In Jorge Luis Borges' celebrated story 'The Aleph', the narrator, drugged and imprisoned in a cellar by a certain Carlos Argentino, finally gets to see the mysterious, long-anticipated Aleph on the nineteenth step of the stairway leading to the cellar. Barely an inch in diameter, the tiny color-shifting ball contains the totality of cosmic space, which embraces all things, and is visible with equal clarity from every conceivable angle. In a hallucinating catalog, the narrator enumerates everything his fevered gaze observes: daybreak and nightfall, the multitudes of America, a silver spider's web in the middle of a black pyramid, a splintered labyrinth, the same tiles in a yard on Soler Street as he'd seen thirty years earlier in the entrance to a house in Fray Bentos, and a great deal more, too much to quote here at length: grapes, snow, tobacco, seams of metal, steam, convex equatorial deserts and their every grain of sand, a circle of dry earth on a sidewalk where a tree had once stood, a summer house in Adrogué, a sunset in Querétaro that seemed to reflect a rose in Bengal, a closet in Alkmaar...

A closet in Alkmaar? Alkmaar in North Holland! My surprised sense of recognition when I read the name may be perfectly explicable, but it quickly makes way for nagging unease. Why get so excited at spotting the word 'Alkmaar'? As ideal reader I should be just as interested in Adrogué and Querétaro as I am in Alkmaar. At the same time, I feel ashamed at my small-mindedness, because the Argentinean cities of Adrogué and Querétaro mean nothing to me, while Alkmaar, on the other hand, is the place in which I grew up. I was born in the city's Wilhelmina Hospital on June 29th, 1957, not far from my parents' house on Juliana van Stolberg Avenue – number 16 – where I was proudly installed a few days later. We moved shortly thereafter to Emma Street 53, where my princely monopoly was challenged by the arrival of a brother. From 1960 we lived a further eight years in Beuken Avenue 8, in the recently constructed Westerhout Park district. On June 29th, 1968, the family left Alkmaar to set up home in another part of the Netherlands, making it eleven years to the day that I had lived in the city. These are historical facts, but the question is: do they mean anything?

My father had been a lawyer in Amsterdam since 1952 and was eager to get started for himself by taking over an existing practice. After some exploratory work he came up with three possibilities: Groningen, Zwolle and Alkmaar. The recently commenced construction of the Velser Tunnel weighted the decision in Alkmaar's favor, since he had little desire to cut himself off in a provincial hinterland. Thanks to the tunnel, therefore, which was finally opened on September 28th, 1957, Alkmaar became the city of my birth, thus enabling Jurjen Vis to include me as the author of poetry, short stories, essays and novels on page 517 of his monumental *Geschiedenis van Alkmaar – History of Alkmaar* under the heading '20th Century Poets and Novelists'.

I set great store by the reference, let it be clear, but it also leaves me a little embarrassed. What can I do in response? I will never be the author of 'The Great Alkmarian Novel' and I'm highly unlikely to pen an epic poem about local heroic resistance against the Spanish oppressors in the 17th century. When it comes to my relationship with the 'city of cheese', I feel a certain kinship with Napoleon Bonaparte: we both left our mark on the city, but we are both – each in his own way – nothing more than a footnote in its history.

NAPOLEON'S CONNECTION WITH ALKMAAR, IF POSSIble even more cursory than mine – is noted as such in the *Alkmaarsche Courant* of October 21st, 1811:

> *Today, around four in the afternoon, we had the good fortune to see His Majesty the Emperor and King pass by. The adjunct mayors and the municipal council with the commandant at arms awaited His Majesty outside the Friese Gate. It pleased*

*His Majesty in his customary goodness to give ear to the claims
presented to him.*

*His Majesty continued his journey in the direction of
Haarlem accompanied by shouts of Long Live the Emperor!
from the assembled crowd. The rest of the day was dedicated to
rejoicing, thanks to the voluntary illumination of the primary
streets and canals.*

These are the historical facts, at any rate the official
version of the facts published under censorship, but the question remains: what do these facts mean? Reality, it seems,
was much more banal, at least as historian E.H.P. Cordfunke
describes it. To begin with, the 'voluntary illumination' was
far from voluntary and had in fact been imposed on the pop-
ulation as early as October 7th by the serving mayor Van
Foreest van Petten. The illumination of the city was an
expensive joke as far as the people were concerned, and the
intended festival atmosphere likewise had to be imposed by
the authorities. The same official announcement also issued
a ban on walking around with guns as Napoleon passed
by and on letting off fireworks. Thoroughfares (such as the
Ritsevoort, Koor Street and Long Street) and streets leading
to the city's gates were to be free of carts and other hin-
drances. It was even forbidden to moor barges under bridges,
presumably for fear of attacks, and the use of the politically
sensitive color orange in street decorations was not permit-
ted. The most detailed regulatory measure was that pots
with flowers and plants were to be located no higher than
five feet above the ground.

In short, the popular revelry that is said to have arisen at the arrival of Emperor Napoleon was far from spontaneous. The city's officials will likewise have been left with few if any cheerful memories of His Majesty's visit. First, there had long been uncertainty as to the date of the impending visit; second, the question arose as to whether the emperor would in fact visit the city at all. The inspection of military fortifications in Den Helder was an appreciably more important reason for the imperial visit to the vicinity than the 'illumination' of Alkmaar's canals, whether voluntary or involuntary. The annexation of Holland into the French empire in 1810 had significantly increased the strategic importance of Den Helder as the 'Gibraltar of the North'.

One can imagine the disappointment of the civic and military authorities, assembled in stately array on October 15th, 1811, next to a special triumphal arch at the city's Kennemer Gate, with a band of musicians and the armed city militia at the ready, when the report arrived that His Majesty preferred first to travel on to Den Helder and then visit Alkmaar two days later on the return journey. The triumphal arch had to be relocated in great haste to the Friese Gate on the north side of the city. But even when the emperor finally arrived with his entourage on October 17th at four in the afternoon, it would have been hard to describe the moment as a visit as such. The gilded key to the city that Alkmaar's dignitaries – who by this time had already been waiting for hours – planned to offer His Majesty with great ceremony was received by Napoleon sitting in his coach with no more than a nod of the head.

G.F. Fontein Verschuir, the sub-prefect of the district of Hoorn in the Department of the Zuiderzee and former mayor of

Alkmaar, had readied his sumptuous – by Alkmaar standards – urban palace on Long Street for a grand reception and had reckoned on serving a meal for sixty guests. Fontein Verschuir had even had a handsome four-poster with damask curtains brought in from Amsterdam to be able to offer His Majesty an appropriate place to rest. But none of it was necessary. The imperial coach only entered the city to change horses and it left the city again in great haste shortly thereafter. The church authorities who had been lined up at the city hall to greet His Majesty will have seen a coach pass by at considerable speed, but they were only informed later that it had been carrying the emperor. The entire imperial visit to the city lasted fifteen minutes at the most. Around six that same afternoon, Napoleon and his entourage had already entered Beverwijk, so that even calling his stay in Alkmaar a 'flying visit' would still be a euphemism. Alkmaar? Napoleon didn't even bother getting out of his coach for the place.

All that remains of this historic visit is the gilded key that had been commissioned a few weeks earlier by the city's optimistic magistrates for the sum of 16.80 francs. Napoleon had clearly not taken it with him. It is supposed to be part of the collection of Alkmaar's Municipal Museum, but the museum's website makes no mention of it. Are the grapes still sour?

AS WAS THE CASE WITH NAPOLEON, MY OWN BRIEF sojourn within the city walls of Alkmaar did not leave much of an impression on local historiography. I too can boast little more than a couple of lines in the same *Alkmaarse Courant*. A short article appeared in the paper on the occasion of a theatre performance at the elementary school I attended. I've lost the clipping, but I still have the photo taken by the well-known Alkmaar photographer Jaap Schoen that accompanied it. In their boundless love and pride, my parents apparently asked for a copy and carefully preserved it. It depicts a circle of excited schoolchildren dancing round a sturdy snowman and throwing snowballs made of crêpe paper at it. My part in the piece, which required incredible endurance, was to play the snowman, a role 'to get wrapped up in' if ever there was one and certainly the 'warmest' performance Alkmaar's theater-goers had ever witnessed.

I freely admit that a minor newspaper reference represents a distinctly humble foundation for the history of my eleven year stay in Alkmaar. Clearly more has to be made of my Alkmaar reminiscences, certainly when compared with the measly fifteen minutes the French emperor spent in the city. If I lie down in the cellar of my memory and stare long enough at the mysterious object on the nineteenth step, perhaps some disconnected images will manifest themselves, images I might catalogue as memories. Let's begin with my earliest memory: a maternity visit to my mother in January 1960 just after my little brother was born. Racing through the living room on my tricycle in the house on Emma Street. The apery and the ever hungry ducklings in the city park. Shaking hands with Santa Claus as crowds of children welcomed him to Alkmaar, far too young to realize that the man behind the beard was in fact the manager of the Eyssen Cheese Factory. Miss Kreijermaat's kindergarten – since burned to the ground – and the elementary Linden School next door where I spent five full years learning to speak the local dialect. Collecting old newspapers in the neighborhood 'for the blind' and using them to light a fire in Alkmaar's Hout Park. The difference between Olga Lodder, the girl I sat next to at school, and Kitty Jongenelen, the beautiful yet unattainable girl at the front of the class who lived on Westerweg and was a cross in my imagination – already distorted by literature – between Rosa Overbeek and Anne Frank. The sea wind that drove the shadows of enormous white clouds across Kastanje Avenue, which I chased as I ran back to the front door of our house on Beuken Avenue, the same as all the other houses on the street, but not quite. Riding in the back of the Volkswagen milk van between the clinking milk bottles. Spartan swimming lessons in the public pool in the early morning winter darkness. The house on Nassau Square where I first ate spaghetti. Brawls, incomprehensible arithmetic, and profoundly dull gymnastics classes at school. Countless walks along the beach near Bergen, Egmond and Schoorl. Uncle Sem from Antwerp who brought me a Mercedes, the only one I'd ever own. Smoking cigarettes in secret. Greengrocer Pool who delivered to the house and had 'Pool's Fruit' on one side of his cart and 'Fine Food' on the other side. Idle days that never ended, filled with the help of a ball, a couple of pebbles or a periscope. Playing with the typewriter in my father's legal office on Broad Street. Football on the patch of grass next to Fritz Conijn Avenue. The smell of mothballs in the hall behind the front door when my grandparents from London came to visit. Watching color TV for the first time at the barber's house. Going camping near St Maartenszee with the Helder family from number

10. Riding pillion on a Zündapp motorbike driven by our housekeeper's husband, a refuse collector, heading off on a fishing trip. Putting nickels on the rails beyond the duckweed covered railway ditch into which I inevitably had to fall one day. Building cabins in the dunes with my father, who always went to work for a couple of hours early on Sunday morning. Cycling during the school holidays with our much loved sitters Aunt Annie and Uncle Jos Keuss when our parents were trying to recover from their children in the Swiss Alps. The last post on the Cheese Market, the Chinese lanterns on November 11th, and the annual carnival on October 8th to remember the expulsion of the Spaniards in 1573. Lodging with the Blauw family at *De Drie Koningshoofden*, the finest, most beautiful farmhouse in Stompetoren. And that time on my English grandfather's lap, steering his 3.5 liter Rover across the immensity of Canada Square.

I peer intensely at the nineteenth step, but the more numerous the things I see in my autobiographical Aleph, the more convinced I become that the details of my personal autobiography are no more and no less useful or interesting than arbitrary facts drawn from the life of another, even the life of the French emperor. It's not so much that I – like Napoleon – look down on the key to the city. It's more that a person has so many keys to choose from. Not only those of Adrogué and Querétaro, but also those of London, Leiden, and Amsterdam, and not to forget Paris, Rome, Athens, Naples, Berlin, New York, Brussels, Barcelona, Stockholm, Prague, Tel Aviv, and Buenos Aires. Why then have the key to the city of your birth gilded? What's important is that you adapt your mind in such a way that it becomes a passkey that lets you in wherever you go. You can return to the city of your birth, of course, but you can also conquer the rest of the world. As emperor or as reader. By comparison, those 'fifteen minutes of obscurity' that both Napoleon and myself spent in Alkmaar – he literally, me figuratively – pale into insignificance.

THREE WAYS
TO BECOME A JEW

On Identity and Freedom

ublishers can be wide of the mark at times, and their blunders always leave a paper trail. Take the letter from the venerable New York publishing house Harcourt, Brace and Company responding to the manuscript of The Assistant, the second novel by Jewish American author Bernard Malamud (1914-1986). Harcourt, Brace had published Malamud's first novel *The Natural* four years earlier on a two-book contract and with reasonable success. Malamud's editor Robert Giroux had transferred in the meantime to the young publisher Farrar, Straus and Cudahy (later Farrar, Straus and Giroux), according to reports because he was disappointed at not being allowed by his bosses to bid on J.D. Salinger's *Catcher in the Rye* (talk about blunders!). What would have been more logical than for Harcourt, Brace to publish the impressive *Assistant* immediately after receiving the manuscript? Given the 'two-book deal' they had earlier concluded with Malamud's literary agent Diarmuid Russell of Russell & Volkening, moreover, the book was already under contract. But John H. McCallum, the publisher at Harcourt, Brace, was of a different mind. He wrote to Malamud's agent on May 31st, 1956:

> *We have come to the reluctant conclusion, after a number*
> *of readings and a great deal of discussion, that we are not*
> *prepared to publish Bernard Malamud's* The Assistant.
>   *There is much that is excellent in this new novel of his,*
> *but on the whole we find it more unsatisfying than satisfying;*
> *we believe it would not be a step upward from* The Natural.

If what McCallum wrote is true, that he and his colleagues had indeed discussed the book at length, then the rejection is all the more curious since even an editorial trainee can see that Malamud's debut *The Natural* may have been a commercially attractive book, no doubt on account of its baseball theme, but that it doesn't hold a candle to *The Assistant*, not even remotely. In fact, it would not be an exaggeration to describe Malamud's second novel as a masterpiece that is not only closer to the author in personal terms, but also reveals the greatness of his pen in the universal development of its theme. *The Assistant* was to sell more than 1.2 million copies on the American market alone in the first twenty years after its publication. But McCallum, son of Catholic missionary parents and a brilliant academic

(Harvard *magna cum laude* and an MA from Columbia), didn't want to touch it. He digs himself deeper into the mire elsewhere in the letter:

I realize this decision may well mean that we shall lose Malamud, and this I regret, for many of us here were and still are enchanted with his first novel. May I say, then, if The Assistant *is not placed with some other publisher, we should be happy to have a chance at his next novel.*

It goes without saying that Harcourt, Brace didn't get that chance. Robert Giroux eagerly welcomed the manuscript at Farrar, Straus and Cudahy, where the book appeared in 1957 and marked the beginning of a collaboration that was to continue for the rest of Malamud's writing career. *The New York Times* praised the clarity and concreteness of the novel's style, the warm humanity he scattered over its characters, the simple immediacy of the important truths that permeate the novel. Forty years after publication, Robert Giroux wrote the following in a letter to me dated May 4th, 1998: '[...] imagine the gall – asking for a chance at "the next novel".' He was clearly still incensed by the infamous letter of rejection from the publishing house to which he himself had dedicated fifteen years of his life, interrupted only by a period of military service.

It is difficult to suppress the thought that the rejection of *The Assistant* by Harcourt, Brace, based on their contention that the novel was 'more unsatisfying than satisfying', had something to do with the book's theme: the ambiguities of

Jewish identity. Without wanting to accuse McCallum posthumously – he died in 2008 – of anti-Semitism (no one, after all, is obliged to publish a brilliant Jewish writer), it's clear that the novel broached a subject that was awkward and even painful in late 1950s New York.

The Assistant tells the story of Morris Bober, a penniless Jewish grocer who is robbed and beaten up in his store one evening by two masked assailants. In spite of the meager ten dollar haul, one of the assailants, Frank Alpine, is consumed with guilt. He quickly returns to the store to work for Bober without pay – at first without revealing his true intentions. His desire to settle his debt, alongside his evolving designs on Bober's cash register and twenty-three year old daughter, sets a series of complications in motion that Malamud develops and interweaves with the hand of a master.

What comes as the biggest shock to the reader, at least the 1950s reader, is not Bober's marginal living conditions, which Malamud – himself the son of a Jewish grocer – portrays with exceptional authenticity. Nor is it the anti-Semitic context in which Bober and his family were expected to eke out their dreary existence. Such phenomena were familiar enough to the American reader. The book's biggest shock is the fact that Frank Alpine, erstwhile assailant, gradually comes to identify with Morris Bober's life, so much so that his atonement, frequent conversations with Bober, and interaction with the man's family lead him by degrees to become ever more Jewish. At the end of the novel, after Bober has died, Alpine decides not only to continue the grocery business, but also to embrace Bober's own fate. He has himself circumcised and becomes a Jew.

This voluntary transformation from non-Jew to Jew was and remains a disquieting reality, if only on account of its unnatural rarity. Millions of Jews down through the centuries have endeavored to ditch their involuntary identity for a safer existence as a non-Jew, shielded from harassment, persecution and even annihilation. And here, in a brilliant twist, Malamud introduces a philo-Semitic ghost driver onto the scene who chooses to head in the opposite direction, against the historical traffic, as a result of what appears to be an entirely logical process.

OF COURSE, MALAMUD WASN'T THE FIRST NOVELIST TO broach the subject of an unnatural transformation from non-Jew to Jew. Ten years earlier, the nowadays forgotten American writer Laura Z. Hobson (1900-1986) caused a major stir with her serialized novel *Gentleman's Agreement*, published in *Cosmopolitan* between November 1946 and February 1947. In this confrontational novel, which appeared in book form on February 27th, 1947, the author, herself the daughter of Russian-Jewish immigrants, introduces a journalist who decides to spend a portion of his life as a Jew. As an angle for a story he is investigating, he thus hopes to acquire and pass on a clearer picture of socially acceptable post-war anti-Semitism in America. The book was a sensation and rapidly found its way to the top of the *New York Times* bestsellers list, with short-term sales reaching one and a half million. It was translated into more than a dozen languages, and published in my native Dutch under the curious title *Ongeschreven wet – Unwritten Law*. The French title *Le mur invisible – The Invisible Wall* was closer to the mark.

As a novel, *Gentleman's Agreement* has since been consigned to oblivion. In stylistic terms it doesn't belong among the literary elite, but as is often the case with skillfully plotted B-novels, the story of a 'voluntary Jew' was transformed into a masterful movie at the hands of the brilliant director Elia Kazan. Gregory Peck played the charming and intelligent journalist Schuyler ('Phil') Green, researching an undercover report entitled 'I Was Jewish for Eight Weeks' exposing the so-called polite anti-Semitism that held sway among the better circles on America's East Coast. Even his ambivalent co-star Kathy (played by Dorothy McGuire), with whom he develops a romantic relationship at the beginning of the film, isn't free of it, although she claims to fully support Green's goals. 'It's detestable, but that's the way it is.' 'Let it alone. You can't write it out of existence.' 'What can one person do?' Kathy's objections and other concerns serve only to reinforce Green's determination to continue his journalistic crusade.

Himself an immigrant, Elia Kazan was all too familiar with the phenomenon of discrimination. He made *Gentleman's Agreement* into a powerful protest movie, which can still elicit moments of shame and awkwardness sixty years after it was first screened. Just as his *America, America* problematized the dream of Anatolian emigration to the US, and his *On the Waterfront* addresses the struggle of dockworkers for a more dignified existence, Kazan's *Gentleman's Agreement* elevated the personal 'problem of Jewish identity' to the status of a universal question facing human society. Starting as a journalistic stunt, Green's disguise gradually becomes second nature: a provisional Jew intent on making the world a better place. At the end of the film, when his co-star Kathy unexpectedly lines up at his side as a militant ally, the two find each other in their shared struggle and in their mutual love.

In combination with the story's happy end, the voluntary and temporary character of the Jewish identity in *Gentleman's Agreement* lets the reader/film audience off easy in a certain sense. After eight weeks of Judaism, 'Phil' Green reverts to the old familiar Schuyler Green. Without further personal confrontation with anti-Semitism, he and Kathy are left to live happily ever after.

SIMILAR CLEMENCY WAS NOT SET ASIDE FOR LAWRENCE Newman, the main character in Arthur Miller's only novel, *Focus*, from 1945, perhaps the most disquieting novel about Jewish identity in American literature and, surprisingly enough, never translated into Dutch. The son of Polish-Jewish immigrants, Miller (1915-2005) penned *Focus* in the final years of the war when he – and ten thousand men like him of every imaginable ethnic background – was working the night shift at the Brooklyn Navy Yard. Echoing the story of Frank Alpine and Schuyler Green, *Focus* is about a non-Jew becoming a Jew. But in contrast to Malamud and Hobson/Kazan, Lawrence Newman's transformation is involuntary. In a mid-1940s New York riddled with implicit and explicit anti-Semitism, Newman, personnel manager of a large corporation, realizes one day that he needs to get himself glasses. His deteriorating eyesight had led him by accident to employ a rather Jewish looking female secretary, which had resulted in a reprimand from his boss. He had tried contact lenses but his eyes refused to tolerate them and the only other option was glasses. But in the process, a counter-miracle takes places: 'Newman' literally becomes a new man. With his new glasses on he suddenly looks pretty Jewish himself.

Far from heroic, the old Newman was more of an 'everyman' type who cherished the same questionable ideas as everyone else. He was inclined to read the anti-Semitic graffiti in the subway with approval, dovetailing perfectly as it did with the semi-explicit ideas that inhabited his own subconscious, and he was always irritated by the behavior and appearance of Jewish fellow passengers. But this worldview is turned inside out from one day to the next. From an insecure, slightly schlemielish non-Jew he is transformed – by the way others look at him and react to him – into an angst-ridden, socially challenged Jew.

With impeccable skill, Arthur Miller manages to imprison his main character in a triangle, the first point of which is formed by his neighbor Fred, a member of the militantly anti-Semitic Christian Front, the second by the local Jewish grocer Finkelstein, a regular target of harassment, and the third by the unfathomable and ethnically ambiguous Gertrude Hart, with whom Newman starts a relationship and then marries. When Newman's trash can is emptied on his lawn for the umpteenth time – as is that of Mr Finkelstein further down the street – and Gertrude presses him to join neighbor Fred's Christian Front to demonstrate that he is genuinely not Jewish, Miller transports the reader into a definitive hell of frantic anxiety and insecurity about what people fear the most: exclusion on every side, complete dispossession of the personal right to exist. In such depths of self-doubt and the annihilation of one's own individuality, it no longer matters what your identity is, if you ever had anything to say about it as a human being in the first place. Driven to the edge by a public assault, which sends Gertrude running, Lawrence Newman decides to report the incident to the local police station. And as the police officer takes down his statement he doesn't even make the effort to deny that he's a Jew.

FRANK ALPINE, SCHUYLER GREEN AND LAWRENCE Newman: a cheat, a do-gooder, and a dope. All three became a Jew in their pursuit of self-realization; the first as a penance, the second out of idealism, the third as a punishment of fate. In the hands of their artistic creators, and setting aside the specific circumstances of time and space, all three are such impressive characters because they come up against the limitations of the human condition. It cannot be denied that for many the 'Jewish experience' in post-war New York may have been extremely problematic, but credit is due to Malamud, Hobson/Kazan, and Miller not so much for their portrayal of the historical period in question, but for the fact that they transformed the problem of Jewish identity into a universally human issue, the problematization of every identity. The eternal question of Jewish identity thus becomes a sort of intensified version of the universal notion that everyone senses a bond with everyone else while at the same time desiring to distinguish themselves from everyone else.

WHEN LAURA Z. HOBSON RECEIVED A MESSAGE FROM The Jewish Book Council in 1947 telling her that her novel

Gentleman's Agreement had been awarded a prize for the best Jewish book, she categorically refused to accept it. She didn't consider her novel to be 'Jewish' in the least, just as she refused throughout her life to be considered and styled a 'woman novelist'. She wasn't a 'Jewish woman writer', but 'a writer, a woman and a Jew'. At the end of her life, however, she publically confessed her regret at having rejected the prize, *nota bene,* in an interview published in the originally Yiddish journal *Forward,* which her radically socialist father Michael Zametkin had helped establish in 1897. Her regret testifies to a level of wisdom that comes with the years. For it's the same with Jewish identity as it is with every other identity: you may be determined to be *who* you are and nothing else, but in the eyes of others you're first and foremost *what* you are.

THE SHIP AND THE CARGO

The Frigate Johanna Maria *as Novel of Ideas*

As a literary genre, the novel of ideas isn't held in high esteem in the Netherlands. It's difficult to avoid the impression that literary critics tend to approach such novels with an added degree of grimness. An undeniable novel of ideas such as Frans Kellendonk's *Mystiek lichaam – Mystic Body*, for example, was accused on publication by one of the most important critics of the day of 'backwardness' and by another of 'anti-Semitism'. To no avail, since the book now stands firm and unassailable as one of the most important Dutch novels of recent decades. The reception of Marcel Möring's work like-wise leaves the impression that the critics were particularly acrid in their assessment of its level of reality – in this instance the plausibility of the narrative – and devoted significantly less energy to the world of ideas contained in his novels (*Het grote verlangen* – *The Great Longing, In Babylon, Dis, Louteringsberg* – *In a Dark Wood*).

The *Van Dale Groot Woordenboek van de Nederlandse Taal* (fourteenth revised edition) – the Oxford or Merriam-Webster of the Dutch world – sets the ball rolling by providing a remarkably pejorative definition of the concept 'novel of ideas': 'a novel in which the narrative is subordinate to the elaboration of an idea'. Such 'subordination' strikes me as nonsense since it suggests that the novel of ideas ultimately falls short as a novel, that the narrative is left to suffer under the weight of its ideas. No one would define a 'historical novel' as one in which the narrative 'is made subordinate' to an account of history. I'm even inclined to see the singular 'idea' as misplaced. I suggest the following improved definition: 'a novel in which the narrative is inextricably linked to the development and elaboration of ideas'.

If we describe the novel of ideas sub-genre in such terms, with a definition that is both broader and more correct, it becomes evident that there are many more novels of ideas within the novel genre than an excessively strict definition would accommodate. I would even maintain that the novel of ideas in literary terms is an ideal to which every novel should ultimately aspire. The definition of a novel as a novel of ideas ought thus, in my opinion, to serve as a criterion of quality for every novel. Put simply, the criterion not only relates to the extent to which an author succeeds in telling a (good) story in his or her novel, but also the extent to which he or she is able to develop (interesting) ideas and carry them across to the reader. And the better a novel succeeds in integrating the development and transfer of ideas into the course of the narrative, so that both streams come across to the reader as one, the more the novel in question will be able to exploit the possibilities of the novel, more so than a book that recounts nothing other than imagined stories about non-existent persons.

The literary ideal of the novel of ideas tends to be sinned against in every conceivable way. Some authors continually interrupt their story for essayistic digressions that leave ugly scars on the surface of the narrative, other novels have characters who wander through their pages as personifications of a certain idea and nothing more, while still other novelists are constantly inclined to explain everything, instead of allowing the ideas incorporated in the book to do their own work. There are also authors who put too few ideas into their novels, leaving readers with the impression that they're listening to the endless stories of a narrator or the similarly endless dialogues of fictional characters. If the novel of ideas is the ideal novel, then the novel without ideas comes close to the lowest imaginable manifestation of lengthier narrative prose. Clearly not the correct approach, but then what is the correct approach? An answer can be found in a careful examination of the form and the content of a novel.

IF WE APPLY THE IDEA CRITERION SUGGESTED ABOVE, then a book that simply has to be included among the absolute top of twentieth-century Dutch novel writing is *Het fregatschip Johanna Maria* – *The Frigate Johanna Maria* by Arthur van Schendel (1874-1946). I would like to claim that this novel is first and foremost a novel of ideas, and only thereafter a historical novel, a sea novel or a realist novel, qualifications normally ascribed to the book. And subjecting *The Frigate Johanna Maria* to the litmus test – the novel of ideas as ideal novel – can help demonstrate why it is such an excellent work.

Published in 1930, Van Schendel's novel tells the story of a man and a ship. The man is Jacob Brouwer, a sail maker living in Amsterdam in the fourth quarter of the nineteenth century, the final heyday of the great Dutch sailing ships that were forced to relinquish their hegemony over the seven seas in face of the speedy advance of maritime steam power in the years around the turn of the century. The ship is the *Johanna Maria*, a three- master launched in the first sentence of the novel – on a day in February 1865 – from a shipyard on Oostenburg Island in Amsterdam. The statue of a woman representing Hope is attached to the bow with the accompanying dictum *Nil desperandum* (Do not despair). A unique understanding between the man and the ship starts to evolve from the very outset. As a result, Jacob Brouwer is able to function as the steersman without the least effort, in spite of the fact that he was trained as a sail maker and nothing else. When he is at the helm, the ship seems lighter and faster, as if it's not sailing through the water but gliding over it. Brouwer knows and understands the ship and possesses – in Van Schendel's words – 'durability of understanding'.

After many years, the exceptional bond between Jacob Brouwer and the *Johanna Maria* inspires Brouwer to explore the possibility of acquiring the ship for himself. On the one hand, the novel recounts his profound tenacity and determination to achieve his goal, and on the other, the unbelievably immense setbacks he encounters in its realization. At one point Brouwer is thrown into prison in Koningsbergen, at another he wakes up in a hospital after a brawl in the port of Honolulu, and at yet another he is abandoned on a barely populated island in the South Pacific. In each instance, 'his' *Johanna Maria* slips through his fingers, because a series of mostly heartless captains set sail without him. But his fidelity to the ship remains and he spends his hard-earned savings looking for the *Johanna Maria*, hoping to find the sometimes pitifully damaged and cold-heartedly treated vessel somewhere in the world. Many a time the ship eludes him only to be rediscovered elsewhere, renamed in succession: *Ingrid, Feodora, Rafaella, Asuncion,* and *Lilian Bird.* After several decades Brouwer is finally able to realize his dream, although by then he and the *Johanna Maria* are both advanced in years. On the novel's concluding page – the first years of the new century – the ship is moored in Amsterdam's Dijksgracht, where it was once launched and observed with much admiration by the then still youthful Brouwer. The elderly Brouwer now lives on board in a sort of introverted duality with his ship, and it is here too that he meets his accidental death on the deck.

SO WHAT ARE THE IDEAS VAN SCHENDEL WANTED TO transmit in and through his story? Let's attempt an inventory: How do people discover their vocation? Where do we find meaning in what we choose as our life's work? Do we choose our life's work or does it choose us? What binds us to the things for which we take responsibility in our lives? What can we lay at fate's door and what not? What does the bond that binds us to the things we possess consist of? Do we already possess something if we dedicate ourselves to it completely? The fulfill-ment of life's deepest desires is often more a tragic reality than reason for triumph. Every life needs a degree of inspiration in order to combat its meaninglessness. Desire as an expression of human deficiency exists for itself alone, we do not choose the object of that desire ourselves, it is determined rather by acci-dent or – if you prefer – by destiny. The perfect performance of a traditional skill can contain a sense of fulfillment equal in completeness to that of a great love. Inanimate objects and tools have a will and a fate equal to that of the people to whom they happen to find themselves entrusted. In the hands of cer-tain people, things can also know happiness. It's even possible to speak of a mutual affinity between things and people: the former suffer with the latter and vice versa. Predestination is a voice that accompanies you throughout your life to which you are obliged to listen. Patience and perseverance are an invin-cible combination. People who do their jobs well and with all their hearts are superior in moral terms to the transitory bosses set above them by accident of money or standing. Every genu-ine human activity conceals an idea that transcends its material dimensions: fidelity, craftsmanship, love, hope, faith, patience and sacrifice all contribute to that activity and constitute its greatest and sometimes only reward. Etc.

It should already be clear from this incomplete list what a wise and inexhaustible book this short novel is. It should also be evident that isolating ideas from a novel of ideas is a perilous and trivializing activity. The themes and questions I have attempted to formulate – no matter how interesting an exercise in itself – seem more like proverbs on wall tiles than real angles of insight into the qualities of the book. In short, it's possible to put a number of ideas in the book into words, but it has to be observed that they thereby lose much of their luster and depth.

The irony of the ideas criterion lies in the following: if one is unable to draw ideas of any importance from a novel in literary terms, the book can be safely set aside without scruples. What we have in this case is an example of so-called '*Unterhaltungsliteratur*' or 'light reading'. If the novel contains interesting ideas that can be ladled out intact and with ease because they're floating about freely within the book without being bound to it in any way, then the novel may be worth its salt but it's not likely to be a masterpiece of the genre. It is only when the said ideas are both present and tangible on every page, chiming along with the characters, with the successive scenes and with the narrative as a whole, but impossible to isolate complete and undamaged, that we can begin to speak of a major novel. In the form of a fictional story, such novels constitute the best and perhaps even the only possible articulation of the ideas they incorporate.

Arthur van Schendel's *The Frigate Johanna Maria* is such a clear and exemplary case in this last category because it is also a relatively short novel containing a little less than 45,000 words. As novels go this is fairly limited. Had it enjoyed the dimensions of Melville's *Moby Dick* or had it been written in English – like Hemingway's even shorter *The Old Man and the Sea* –, the book would have had a much greater chance of securing an international reputation. Indeed, even today there are nine or ten translations of the book in circulation. In the Netherlands, however, it has suffered for decades from a relative lack of interest, reprinted from time to time in omnibus editions, but usually only available as an independent work in second hand bookshops. For one reason or another, *The Frigate Johanna Maria* hasn't found its way into any of the canonical lists. Perhaps that has to do with its diminutive size, with Van Schendel's abbreviated, 'scenario' style of writing. Surely such a style would be a help more than a hindrance nowadays, a positive advantage, but it seems that either Van Schendel's pre-war neo-romantic reputation is still too off-putting for contemporary readers or his attraction as a literary figure is no longer sufficient, unlike Louis Couperus, for example, whose work nowadays makes a much more 'nineteenth century' impression.

If, as I suggest, *The Frigate Johanna Maria* ought to be understood in the first instance as a novel of ideas, then its modest literary status serves to illustrate the lack of Dutch appreciation for this type of writing. The novel itself cannot be reasonably blamed for this neglect, since *The Frigate Johanna Maria* is one of the finest 'small but big' novels of twentieth-century Dutch literature, Dutch to the core and utterly universal at one and the same time. The ship and its cargo do not contradict one another in Van Schendel's book, rather they form a perfect synthesis.

A FALSE DAWN

Oscar Wilde Before and After May 20ᵗʰ, 1897

Three times in his life, Oscar Wilde stood on the deck of a ship that was about to tie up at a port that would herald a new experience for the writer, ushering in an entirely new phase in his life. On April 3ʳᵈ, 1877, as a twenty-two year old student in the company of Irish archaeology Professor John Pentland Mahaffy and two other students, he watched the sun go down from the deck of a ship as it approached the port of Katakolon. Shortly thereafter he set foot on Greek soil for the first time, an event he immediately immortalized in the sonnet 'Impression de voyage'. On January 2ⁿᵈ, 1882, the twenty-seven-year-old dandy Oscar Wilde watched from the deck as the SS *Arizona* sailed into the port of New York, where he was to start a year-long tour of America, giving lectures and interviews and enjoying considerable social success. And in the early morning of May 20th, 1897, Wilde stood on the forward deck of the ferryboat *La Tamise* as it sailed from Newhaven to Dieppe, embracing exile and turning his back on England forever after two full years in British jails. Under his arm he was carrying a large sealed envelope containing the manuscript of a work that was to gain fame and notoriety under the title *De Profundis*, a work he wrote behind bars. Of these three dates, the third is the most intriguing because it reveals such a fine mixture of promising and ill-fated elements. As such, May 20th, 1897 can serve as a threshold, as a symbol for the great paradox that dominated Oscar Wilde's life: how a brilliantly gifted master of the art of living acquired global renown with the disintegration of his existence as a writer and as a human being.

He had been released from London's Pentonville Prison early the previous day, but instead of travelling to France without delay he spent the entire day shilly-shallying in the company of his good friend More Adey at the house of the Reverend Stewart Headlam, who had unselfishly stood bail for him in 1895, allowing him to prepare in freedom for his second and decisive trial. His faithful friend, the writer Ada Leverson, came to visit him in his regained freedom with her husband Ernest. There was much to discuss, and freedom itself must have been well-nigh overwhelming. What would he do? Where should he go? In his confusion he even sent a message to the Jesuits of the Church of the Immaculate Conception in Farm Street, Mayfair, asking if they would receive him for a six-month retreat. The Jesuits informed him by return of post that such a retreat required a year of preparation, to which Wilde responded by bursting into tears, exhausted as he was after two years of incarcerated sleeplessness, hunger, and a slew of physical ailments.

Spent in the company of friends and well-intentioned acquaintances, May 19th passed as irresolutely as the day Wilde was arrested close to two years earlier on April 5th, 1895. The two dates are perfect mirror images of one another. Wilde had lost the case brought against him by the father of his young friend Lord Alfred Douglas. There had been witnesses enough to prove that Douglas' father, the Marquess of Queensberry, had rightly branded Wilde in public as someone who 'behaved like a Sodomite' ('posing as Somdomite' as Queensberry misspelled the word on a visiting card in his rage). In the course of a number of hearings, so many incriminating statements concerning Wilde's sexual conduct came to the surface that everyone who was well-disposed towards him strongly advised him to leave the country without delay. 'The detestable and abominable vice of buggery', as homosexuality had been known for centuries in England where it was an indictable offence, was not a crime in France, for example. But with a strange amalgamation of fatalism, indecision, and bravura, Oscar Wilde chose to defend the life he had led and the love that was an inseparable part thereof. In the afternoon of April 5th, 1895, he was arrested without the slightest resistance in his room at the Cadogan Hotel, where he had spent several hours waiting for the inevitable. His proud pigheadedness gave rise to two impressive trials, with cross-examinations that were to make both legal and literary history, but for Wilde himself there was only martyrdom in the form of a two-year jail sentence with hard labor delivered on May 25th, 1895.

The self-declared 'King of Life' thus had to exchange his glorious life as the most successful playwright of his day – with midnight suppers, willing boys, and 'life for art's sake' – for two years in a cell with wooden planks for a bed, meals of gruel with brown prison bread and potatoes with suet pudding, filling his days pointlessly picking oakum from old tarred ropes. *An Ideal Husband* and *The Importance of Being Earnest*, the two most recent of Wilde's enormously successful society comedies were immediately struck from theatre repertoires or consigned to the provinces without his name attached. His library and other household items were sold by auction in front of his house on Tite Street, Chelsea, for ridiculously low prices. He was left in his cell to fret over the humiliation and the irreparable ruination of his family night after sleepless night. Repeated attempts to have his sentence shortened were unsuccessful. Oscar Wilde was forced to sit out the entire two years of the sentence imposed on him.

Now, Wilde had to reinvent himself and give new direction to his life. His friends, were certain of one thing: the writer had to leave England. He was too controversial, his social position was unsustainable, his prospects as a writer non-existent. If anywhere offered the promise of a new existence it was on the other side of the Channel. So in the days prior to his release, faithful friends Robert Ross and Reginald Turner, together with More Adey, made the necessary arrangements for his passage to France.

Wilde finally sent a telegraph from Newhaven at 6:25 pm the previous evening after the noon ferry had long departed:

'Arriving by night boat. [...] You must not dream of waiting up for us. In the morning we will meet. Please engage rooms for us at your hotel.' On May 20th Robert Ross and Reginald Turner waited in the early hours for the arrival of the night ferry from England. It promised to be a soft spring day, but at four thirty in the morning the sun had not yet risen, and shielded as it was from the sea, the port of Dieppe where the ferry was expected to put in was still entirely shrouded in the half-light of dawn.

Intended as a foreword to an edition of Wilde's letters that never appeared as such, Robert Ross later described Wilde's arrival in French exile as follows:

> *When the steamboat slipped into port, the figure of Wilde, which stuck out above the other passengers, was easy to recognize from the huge crucifix on the pier where we were standing. This conspicuous beacon was full of meaning for us. Then we started to run towards the landing stage and Wilde recognized us, waved to us and his lips curled into a smile.*

After the usual customs formalities, Oscar Wilde and More Adey disembarked onto Quai Henri IV. 'This, my dear Bobby, is the great manuscript about which you know,' Wilde solemnly announced to Robert Ross, pointing to the envelope under his arm after the friends had exchanged greetings. The four made their way to Hotel Sandwich, where Wilde signed in under the pseudonym Sebastian Melmoth – a reference to the martyrdom of Saint Sebastian and to the central character in the novel *Melmoth the Wanderer* written by his great-uncle Charles Maturin – thereby formalizing his new existence. The men chatted for hours until at 9 am everyone, with the exception of Wilde, decided to indulge themselves in a couple of hours sleep, exhausted from the early start. They lunched together at twelve, during which Wilde was finally able to exercise his familiar conversational talents anew after his lonely sojourn behind bars.

In the afternoon, the four friends headed inland by coach to the small town of Arques-la-Bataille, roughly four miles from the hotel, where they continued their conversation at the foot of the medieval town wall. Wilde, of course, had a great deal to say about the hardships he underwent in a succession of prisons, and he spoke with praise and even affection of Major Nelson, the director of Reading Prison. In the final months of his incarceration, Nelson gave him free rein to work on the prison manuscript, which the author himself had entitled *Epistola: In Carcere et Vinculis*. Wilde likewise had much to say about the impressions now flooding his 'reborn' senses: the sight of the sea, the smell of the grass and the trees on this magnificent spring day, the sounds of French country life.

What Wilde and his companions did the rest of that afternoon – a drink in Dieppe at Café Suisse or Les Tribunaux, both on the Grand Rue, or dinner in Hotel Sandwich or elsewhere – is unknown to us. But even without a precise hour by hour reconstruction, May 20th, 1897, must certainly qualify as a crucial day in the life and literary career of Oscar Wilde.

It will have been tangible, in the first place, in the long-awaited sense of perfection that for Wilde must have prevailed that day. After all the pain, discomfort and deprivation of imprisonment, he was finally enjoying a glorious spring day in the best possible company of three dear friends. While he was never to see England again, the forty-two-year-old writer will have recovered a certain degree of trust that day in his creative and social potential, his conversational talents and his physical condition. He will have cherished the hope that a future had been set aside for him on the European continent, a new career as a writer, a new life. He had money problems, unquestionably, and was deeply saddened by the irrevocable – in all probability – separation from his two children, but on that sun-drenched spring day on the French coast he also made new and valuable discoveries, the possibility of an existence that was much simpler and more genuine than the artificial, unrealistic and sensational social life he had lived in the years prior to his conviction.

Part of the tragedy of that May 20th lies in the fact that his friends had to return home after a few days, leaving Wilde alone, surrounded by English holidaymakers who quickly realized who he was and did not exactly react with kindness to the discovery. And the highly social Wilde clearly had no talent for loneliness, especially after the overdose he had endured in the preceding two years. Based on the divorce agreement between himself and his ex-wife, he was not allowed to associate with 'disreputable persons', and if he did he would lose his allowance of £3 per week. 'Disreputable person' par excellence was his friend Lord Alfred Douglas, sixteen years his younger and deeply embroiled in the tragedy of Wilde's conviction for 'gross indecency'.

Oscar Wilde endured the loneliness for a couple of weeks, first in Dieppe and from May 27th in Hotel de la Plage in Berneval to the north where he rented a small villa – Chalet Bourgeat – a short while later. His free but incredibly solitary existence was only interrupted by rare and occasional visits from friends and fellow writers. With the exception of *The Ballad of Reading Gaol*, most of which was written in Berneval, he produced little more than a few articles about the English prison system submitted to the editor of *The Daily Chronicle* and a stream of letters to friends and acquaintances in which money – or the lack thereof – formed a recurring motif.

The first letter he wrote to Alfred Douglas after his release is dated June 2ⁿᵈ, 1897, only days after he moved to Berneval, and a reunion with his beloved 'Bosie' most probably took place in Rouen on August 28ᵗʰ of the same year. 'Do remake my ruined life for me', he wrote to Bosie shortly after the reunion, 'and then our friendship and love will have a different meaning to the world.' And Douglas himself later wrote: 'Poor Oscar wept when I met him at the station. We walked the entire day arm in arm, or hand in hand, and our happiness was complete.'

History repeats itself here in a certain sense: Wilde couldn't live without Douglas, but life *with* him required fresh sacrifices both emotionally and financially. To avoid burdening the relationship with Douglas any further, Wilde banished the prison manuscript he had handed to Ross completely from his mind. The question still remains whether Douglas ever received this lengthy prison letter in whatever form, in spite of the fact that it was addressed to him, but there can be little doubt that he had not read it in its entirety at the time. The autobiographical text was only to appear – in a mutilated form – in 1905, five years after Wilde's death on November 30ᵗʰ, 1900. Only in 1912 did Douglas learn of the complete catalogue of accusations Wilde had included in his letter. Douglas had started libel proceedings in that year against the author of a biography of Wilde, and the author in question had asked for Wilde's entire prison letter to be read out in court to corroborate some of the statements he had made about Douglas in his book. Douglas died in 1945, the remainder of his life poisoned by what he heard that day.

But there was no trace of such later events and posthumous misery on that beautiful spring day in May 1897. For Oscar Wilde, May 20th, 1897, held the promise of a new life in freedom, a new identity under a new name, a new fatherland that accepted and respected him as he was, where his books were translated and published and judged exclusively according to their artistic merits. That day was marked by the unspoiled pleasure of a reunion with three of his best friends and the promise of resuming his writing career. But May 20th, 1897 was a 'false dawn' in the life and writing career of Oscar Wilde, a dawn almost like twilight starting to fall over the remaining three and a half years of his life. It's difficult to say that he sincerely believed in that dawn, but he must certainly have enjoyed it to the full. In any case, sincerity was never his strongest feature. One might even dare to claim that he considered sincerity to be more of a vice than a virtue, an attitude that can no doubt be appreciated in an artist, although it ultimately ruined his life as a husband, father, and lover. On May 20th, 1897, a new spring sun spread its light over the life and writing career of Oscar Wilde, but its salutary warmth was to be short-lived. The date thus represents a strip of light between the shadows of his complex past and the murky prospects of an impending early death.

NEUTRALITY VERSUS ENGAGEMENT

Writers as Soldiers

'The day before Dennis left, he wrote a letter to his parents. Writing to the people we love before we go on a journey is a common enough occurrence, especially as none of us has a crystal ball. But for twenty-three-year-old first lieutenant Dennis van Uhm, this was a particularly special letter. In March 2008, he left for Uruzgan in Afghanistan as platoon commander of the 45th Armored Infantry Battalion. On April 18th, 2008, he was traveling in an open jeep as part of a convoy when he drove over a so-called 'homemade' bomb. He and soldier first class Mark Schouwink both lost their lives.

I don't know the precise content of Dennis's letter, although his father quoted from it during a press conference. Coincidence would have it that his father, Peter van Uhm, was installed as Commander of the Royal Netherlands Armed Forces on the day before his son died. He told journalists that the letter Dennis wrote to his parents was explicitly intended to address the eventuality that something might happen to their son.

It appears that extensive media interest in the death of Van Uhm Jr., and his father's press conference a couple of days later, inspired many Dutch soldiers serving on the peace mission to Afghanistan to write similar letters. In the event that a soldier should lose his life, those left behind would have some final words of farewell, written by their loved ones in the knowledge that what they wrote could never be changed or added to.

Such farewell letters not only place demands on the sincerity, charity, and character of those who write them, they also put their linguistic and creative skills to the test. At the moment of writing, choosing the words ultimately intended to replace the author of such a letter in as yet hypothetical circumstances, whether proximate or remote, seems a virtually impossible task.

In essence, however, this is precisely the challenge every author has to face: to write something in such a way that it has the capacity to replace or survive its author, sooner or later. From this perspective, the farewell letter of a soldier is one of the most intense documents a person can write, only comparable in terms of intensity with the last words of a suicide, the final request of someone condemned to the gallows, or the letter to a lover ending a relationship. When our life is in danger, facing an unavoidable end, or forced to endure definitive separation, we are transformed into the words we write. Flesh becomes word. It is hard to imagine a more profound engagement with language.

FRENCH LITERATURE INCLUDES DOZENS OF EXAMPLES
of writers who thus addressed a letter to their loved ones at the
height of a historical emergency in their lives to express their
attitude to life in the face of potential death. The First World
War alone witnessed the death of more than five hundred
greater and lesser French writers whose names are immortalized – according to national custom – in the Panthéon:
Charles Péguy, Henri Barbusse, Alain-Fournier, Jacques Vaché,
Guillaume Apollinaire, Victor Segalen and many more. They
left letters, many written from the front, addressed to wives,
fiancées, friends, and parents, as well as poems and diaries.
The Panthéon also includes the names of roughly two hundred
authors who died in the Second World War. All told, the situation in France testifies to a catalogue of literary and patriotic
engagement that is barely conceivable from the perspective of
Dutch literary history, an engagement that is almost, if not completely, absent in the Netherlands.

At least two reasons can be proposed to explain the difference. In the first instance, the Netherlands maintained as strict as
possible a policy of neutrality in the hundred years prior to 1939,
i.e. the period in which nationalism in Europe led to numerous
and massive armed conflicts. The idea of successive Dutch gov-
ernments was that the absence of alliances with other powers
would ensure that such conflicts would not come knocking on
our national door. This national option for 'non-engagement' has
its counterpart – and this is the second reason – in the attitude of
Dutch literary writers and poets, which can be characterized as
a systematic aloofness and a preponderant obsession with the linguistic, the psychological, the experimental, in short the artistic

dimension of writing. The debate opened by literature professor Ton Anbeek in the 1980s, asking contemporary Dutch writers for more 'streetwise' literary fiction, and revived more recently by his younger colleague Thomas Vaessens, can only be fully understood against the background of our national history. In this recurring debate about the 'streetwisdom' of Dutch letters, it would therefore be advisable to pay more attention to the history of Dutch nineteenth-century literature.

A handful of giant literary personalities that represent an exception to the image of the period 1839-1939 thus sketched (in particular Multatuli, Busken Huet, Ter Braak and Huizinga) confirm the wise proverbial rule. It was only in the 1930s, when history knocked loud and clear on the Dutch national door, that engagement ultimately became unavoidable and finally manifested itself in Dutch literature.

IN HIS DEBUT COLLECTION *HET GEVECHT MET DE MUZE – Fighting the Muse*, published in February 1940 in the Helikon series, the Catholic neo-romantic poet Bertus Aafjes' famous sonnet heralded an ominous onrush of events:

THE LAST LETTER
The world seemed full of brighter sounds
as in his overcoat a sleeping soldier dreamed,
smiling at the peace or so it seemed
because a bell was ringing all around.

A bird, that was no bird, fell on the land
amid the sundrenched herbs, not far away

and never did he rise for green gave way
to red, which every man will understand.

Then o'er the gray horizon once again
there rumbled through the wind and rain
the sounds of distant canon - kind at heart.

But while so still he lay there from his coat
a page unfurled itself, the last he wrote:
My sweet, they say the war is yet to start.

But before the ink of that sublime last line was well and truly dry, war and occupation had become a reality for the Netherlands as well. From that moment on, national neutrality and personal aloofness were no longer possible. From 1940 to 1945 their place was taken by a malicious antithesis between 'right' and 'wrong' writers, the Dutch word for the latter – *fout* – being synonymous with collaboration, and after the liberation followed decades of acrimonious score-settling with those among our men and women of letters who had registered with the Nazi-established *Kultuurkamer* during the occupation. For many Dutch authors, the sudden necessity to engage against the Nazis was too much of a strain on the conscience.

After the war, the Netherlands opted unequivocally for an alliance with its liberators, primarily in the form of NATO membership. But what happened to our writers and poets? They scurried with haste to adopt stances of various sorts: against government policy on the Dutch East Indies, against Dutch military interventions to prevent decolonization, against the 'cultural mandarins', and later against the war in Vietnam, against the establishment or against the stationing of nuclear weapons on Dutch soil. The right-wrong schism that emerged during the German occupation seemed to have spurred on a post-war engagement whereby Dutch literature finally signed itself up for European modernity, although it was clearly in no hurry to do so. While Gerrit Kouwenaar's 1951 novel *Ik was geen soldaat – I Was Not a Soldier* is not autobiographical, its title can be interpreted as almost programmatic for the mental climate that pervaded post-war Dutch literature: protest but don't fight.

It has to be said, of course, that many Dutch writers and intellectuals fell victim to oppression, imprisonment, and discrimination during the German occupation. Through persecution and personal martyrdom, moreover, diarists like Anne Frank, David Koker, and Philip Mechanicus each provided a unique chronicle of the exceptional crimes committed against the Dutch Jews in the years between 1940 and 1945. This does not alter the fact, however, that it's difficult to think of a literary figure who actually took up arms here in the Netherlands in defense of freedom and against the occupation. Hispanicist Johan Brouwer (1898-1943) and writer and artist Willem Arondéus (1894-1943) certainly deserve a mention in this regard. They paid for their celebrated attack on Amsterdam's office of records with death by German firing squad. The attack, in which several other underground militants participated, is all the more celebrated because it is alas a rare example of active, armed resistance against the occupier in which writers were involved.

IS THERE SUCH A THING AS A NATIONAL DISPOSITION
that characterizes the inhabitants of a country and thus also the
mentality of its governing and intellectual elite? Not a snapshot
of a particular spirit of the times or an intellectual movement
that manages to capture a given generation, but a sustained
characterological watermark on the basis of which one can
distinguish a Dutch person from an inhabitant of Germany,
Britain, or France, whether it be 1839, 1939, or 2013? If it's a
question of patriotic 'willingness to die', then an evident conti-
nuity can be observed in the last one hundred and fifty years of
Dutch history. A clear line can be traced from the Ten Days'
Campaign in 1831 against Belgian separatists, in which, with
the exception of a few companies of students and a couple of
thousand Frisians, the majority of those who fought were individuals of questionable social character pressed into serving in
the army, all the way to the end of obligatory military service in
1997, which for many was to be avoided at whatever cost.

One of the events on the twentieth-century European
political stage that *did* profoundly inspire a number of Dutch
writers and artists was the Spanish Civil War. In addition to
Johan Brouwer, writers, journalists, and filmmakers such as
Albert Helman, Anton Constandse, Arthur Lehning, and Joris
Ivens engaged themselves from 1936 onwards with the business
of resisting General Franco and supporting Spanish liberty. It
would appear that the long sustained Dutch neutrality was no
longer an acceptable point of departure for such individuals
in light of the international political situation. A total of *circa*
seven hundred Dutch International Brigade volunteers even
ran the risk of losing their Dutch nationality by serving in a

foreign army. They also wrote history in doing so, a history that deserves a more thoroughly researched and, above all, more prominent place in biographies and studies.

THE WRITER JEF LAST (1898-1972) SURELY COUNTS AS A remarkable Dutch literary figure who responded to the appeal of defending the ideal of a free Spain. Shortly after his return from a disappointing visit to the Soviet Union in the company of André Gide, Last headed off in September 1936 to spend a period of more than a year at the Spanish front, motivated by his sense of adventure and strong ideological convictions. The trip didn't include much sleeping in his overcoat like the soldier in Aafjes' sonnet. The Spanish Civil War was an unforgiving reality that repeatedly tested Last's convictions. Nevertheless, an almost boyish sense of excitement can also be discerned in the letters he wrote to his wife from Spain, initially published in the collection *Brieven uit Spanje – Letters from Spain* (1936). The reader is able to sense that the author clearly takes pleasure in being in the middle of history as he puts it, in being a part of crucial world events. Perhaps his frenetic mentality also conceals an elevated awareness of his own destiny. After all, it was not beyond the bounds of possibility that he might meet his end in far off Spain fighting for a more just world.

THIS SENSE OF POTENTIALLY FATAL IDEALISM, A FEELing that evidently has the power to arouse uncommonly vital energies, is handsomely expressed by Vik de Wildt, the main character in the novel *Soldaat in Uruzgan – Soldier in Uruzgan* written by Dutch army major Niels Roelen and published in

2009 with a foreword by Arnon Grunberg. De Wildt says: 'To be honest, I never felt more alive than I did when I thought I was going to die.' From the artistic perspective, such a statement has little meaning: at the end of the day, the precise personal experiences of the author do not matter one way or the other for a literary text. But from the human perspective, an un-Dutch mentality is evident here, a mentality that has something attractive about it. The same can be said for Jef Last's war letters. In other words, the style of his descriptions might seem inflated to the modern reader, his aesthetic at times questionable, but the ethics they conceal is worthy of praise. If these letters from the Spanish front had not been written by Jef Last, but by an American soldier who had experienced D-Day and was on his way north to liberate the Netherlands from the Krauts, then we would be inclined to read them with respect and gratitude. Isn't it a telling and slightly sad statement about the moral state of Dutch literature that a literary soldier such as Jef Last no longer enjoys a reputation in his own country, that little if any reference is ever made to his work, and that none of it has been available in print for years?

In a letter from Madrid dated November 2nd, 1936, Last writes to his wife Ida:

While I was working on my report about the state of Madrid we were informed unexpectedly from barracks that we would be going back to the front the following morning, i.e. today. Since I was expected at barracks at 9 am, I got up at 6 to make time to write. The days in Madrid have flown by. After the hardships of the front, suddenly a guest room in the former palace of

*the Duke of Herida Spinola. Best of all, a room all to myself to
work in. I've written so much and expect to write so much more
in circumstances like this! [...]*

*Our departure isn't entirely unexpected. The first, second
and fourth company already set off yesterday, singing as they
marched magnificently in step. Wives and mothers lined the
pavements and greeted them with clenched fists. A battalion
like this marching through a neighborhood is almost exclusively
made up of men from the neighborhood itself. Young boys march
a distance beside their departing brothers. Red banners or flags
hang from every house, no matter how poor. The sense of pride
is so joyous, so splendid, that the remaining battalions are
jealous of their departing comrades. The desire to return to the
front is a fever in everyone's blood. To finally settle scores! To
finally crush fascism. No pasaran!*

In the context of Dutch literature, such a letter is a rare
expression of active engagement, an engagement in which the
literary goes hand in hand with a militant humanism, written by someone for whom creativity and activism were not
mutually exclusive. The question remains: is such a disposition simply un-Dutch and is our historical Dutch neutrality
firmly back in the saddle nowadays, or is there a latent engagement among Dutch writers that is ready to spring into action
when push comes to shove? One should not say this out loud,
of course, but would the entire Dutch literary world – with no
exceptions, myself included – not perhaps benefit from being
subjected to this moral test one day? Who then would emerge
as our literary heroes?

THE CONSCIOUSNESS OF ITALY

On Heinrich Schliemann and Sigmund Freud

What's obligatory in Italy? Nothing! It's one of the country's most attractive features: you don't have to do anything, and you can wriggle out of more or less everything. There's nowhere in the world where *dolce far niente* – *carefree idleness* is so self-evident than the land that invented the expression. And even if this is a cliché or completely untrue, the fact remains that down through the centuries countless moneyed bon viveurs and other good-for-nothings have made their way there in search of a more luxurious, gentler, more paradisiacal existence. By tradition, artists and writers appear to follow a similar inner compass that drives them to Italy. The hordes of painters, artists, poets, essayists, and novelists who have travelled to Italy in the last few centuries for shorter or longer stays, many on the brink of adulthood, others later, would be well-nigh impossible to list. Some felt so at home after their arrival that a return to their former existence became impossible. Italophile John Ellingham Brooks summarized it best, when speaking about his discovery of the island of Capri: 'I came for lunch and stayed for life.'

Irony would have it, however, that when they land in Italy the majority of artists and writers do not opt to do nothing, but prefer on the contrary to go to work like people possessed, armed with the multitude of new impressions the country has to offer them. Those who set foot in Rome for the first time, cast a virgin eye over Venice, or absorb the previously unseen vistas of Umbria or Tuscany are likely to be overwhelmed. It is not without reason that medical science has even identified a condition arising from an overexposure to aesthetic sensations, a disorder that goes by the name of 'Stendhal Syndrome'. A visit by the French author to the city of Florence in 1817 was so overpowering that the very sight of all the beauty he beheld literally made him ill.

But very soon after the first confrontation, the creative personality will start to do everything in its power to cope with this endless stream of historical, artistic, and scenic impressions. Thousands of writers, artists, and students – later backpackers, train tourists, and hitchhikers – have sought to compensate in books, drawings, paintings, photos, letters, and blogs for their impotence in the face of such an enormous serving of beauty, natural magnificence, and cultural opulence. Forget *dolce far niente*; Italy is an endless and uncompromising incentive to invent and make things, to remember and fantasize, to make love with its art and history.

You would almost think that the 'inner compass' that has driven artists to Italy for centuries follows some kind of pattern, that the ancient and historical discoveries that lie in wait for the potential visitor must be connected in one way or another with the human consciousness. Such a speculative idea is worth checking with the man who discovered consciousness.

MOST PEOPLE HAVE NO IDEA WHAT THEIR LIVER LOOKS like, a fact that the Dutch writer J.M.A. Biesheuvel introduced into one of his stories to question whether he in reality possessed such an organ. We likewise tend to have little if any idea about the shape of our stomach or our kidneys. There is actually only one internal organ in the human body for which a more or less precise representation has circulated for centuries among painters, graphic artists and illustrators, and that is the heart. A child of three is able to draw it. Nevertheless, all those countless images do not even come close to the reality of the human heart: a blue-veined, blood-soaked lump of flesh. You wouldn't even recognize your own heart if you encountered it in the trash.

In addition to our physical organs, there is a second component of the human morphology that acquired initial form in the last quarter of the nineteenth century, namely consciousness. Sigmund Freud – its discoverer – pictured human consciousness as a layered phenomenon, an entity with a superego (Über–Ich) on top, consciousness – at the level of daily reality – in the middle, and a hidden mental life underneath (subconscious) in which dreams, fears, jokes, frustrations, memories and suppressed events lead a secret existence. Taken together, these layers do not yet provide a clear shape, but they at least offer some initial steps in the process of visualizing the human psyche.

Freud based his spatial presentation of the human consciousness on the discoveries of the German archaeologist Heinrich Schliemann, whose great book *Ilios* provided a detailed – layer by layer – account of the past of the city of Troy, hitherto considered to have been mythical. Remarkably, Schliemann precedes his archaeological descriptions with a – albeit *avant la lettre* – Freudian autobiographical story in which he adds a searching self-analysis of his origins and life history to the self-excavated temporal layers.

For Freud, born in 1856, reading Schliemann's *Ilios* – originally published in 1881 – was a revealing experience and was to profoundly influence the way he thought. He had been fascinated for some time by widespread press reports of Schliemann's archaeological discoveries in Troy and Mycenae and bought the book for himself in May 1899. It is clear from a letter to Wilhelm Fliess that he enjoyed the book immensely, especially the introductory exposé recounting Schliemann's early years and upbringing. After reading the book, Freud started to model certain details of his own life on Schliemann's autobiography: poor background, lonely struggle for recognition, and the feeling of being chosen by fate. But the greatest influence Schliemann exercised on Freud is to be found in the published works of the Viennese psychiatrist.

Freud expressed his indebtedness to the archeological conceptual model in several places in his work. The first specific reference to archeology can be found in his *Studies on Hysteria* from 1895 (written with Josef Breuer), in which he speaks about scraping away psychological material layer by layer and makes a comparison with the excavation of a buried city. A year later, in a lecture delivered to the Viennese *Verein für Psychiatrie und Neurologie* – Psychiatry and Neurology Association on April 21st, 1896, Freud explicitly deploys the archeological metaphor as a legitimation of the new science of psychoanalysis. In the decades that followed he was to exploit the parallel between both – almost equally new and similarly begrudged a place in 'genuine' scientific circles – disciplines repeatedly. Towards the end of his life, Freud wrote the following in his 1937 treatise *Constructions in Analysis*: '[...] just as the archaeologist builds up the walls of the building from the foundations that have remained standing, determines the number and position of the columns from depressions in the floor, and reconstructs the mural decorations and paintings from the remains found in the debris, so does the analyst proceed when he draws his inferences from the fragments of memories, from the associations, and from the behavior of the subject of the analysis.'

What makes this presentation of the human consciousness as a three-dimensional space in which the remains of everything a person ever thought or experienced are waiting, as it were, to be excavated, so elegant is that such a space is also an accumulation of temporal elements. On close inspection, every archaeological layer in the human consciousness alludes to a particular period in time. The present is on top, the past below, and at the very bottom one encounters the hidden memories of youth that represent the earliest phase of the human individual. Or as Freud himself put it in a letter to Sergei Pankejeff, alias 'the Wolfman': 'The psychoanalyst, like the archaeologist, must uncover layer after layer of the patient's psyche, before coming to the deepest, most valuable treasures.' And for Freud, like Schliemann, the results of the 'excavations' were the most important issue. Scientific justification thereof was supported where necessary by careful (re) arrangement of the results and by a flamboyant narrative presentation. From the very outset, the publicity attracting genius with which Schliemann managed to confirm his reputation as the father of archaeology was seductively inspiring for Freud. The journalistic adage 'never let the facts get in the way of a good story' can be applied with justification to the methods employed by both of these pioneers.

FREUD'S INTEREST IN ARCHAEOLOGY WAS BROAD: FROM the Acropolis to the Trojan excavations and from Sir Arthur Evans' Minoan discoveries in Crete to Mycenae. His everyday life also reflected this fascination. At the age of forty, and shortly after returning from his first visit to the Mediterranean region, he started to collect antiquities, art works, ethnographic material, and other (pre)historical objects, an activity that was ultimately to evolve into a collection of roughly two thousand items, making his office in Vienna seem more like an archaeologist's study than a doctor's consulting room. But Freud's primary fascination was for Italy, the buried treasures of Pompeii and in particular the city of Rome. In Italy, and especially in the eternal city, he encountered a jumble of ruins – temples, palaces, baths, fortresses, gates – that was almost impossible to disentangle. The said remains were not only the product of artists, architects, and rulers, they also formed a visible tableau exposing, as it were, thousands of years of history. In his *Das Unbehagen in der Kultur* – *Civilization and its Discontents* from 1930, Freud referred to the city of Rome as the preeminent place in which we can see 'how history is preserved'; not how the past *was*, but how the past *is*. In a historical vision, he goes on to describe the city as a 'mental entity' with a long and rich past, 'in which nothing once constructed had perished, and all the earlier stages of development had survived alongside the latest.'

NO ONE IS LIKELY TO INSIST THAT SIGMUND FREUD'S psychoanalytic interpretations and therapies are capable of withstanding scholarly critique at every level. Many even are no match to simple common sense. But from my perspective, Freud's picture of Italy as a constellation of space and time in which everything and every era exist simultaneously serves as a possible explanation for the country's all-embracing, inexhaustible, and overwhelming power of attraction. It is for this precise reason, that Italy is such an ideal (art-)historical *Fundgrube* – *treasure chest* and at the same time a mirror in the present for writers and artists.

In the wake of earlier (grand) tourists, present-day visitors still experience Italy, more than any other Mediterranean country, as appealing not only to their aesthetic sensitivities and awareness of history, but also to their life thus far, their historical baggage, their self-image, their future ideals, in short their entire personality with all its already formed and yet to be explored experiences. It is perhaps for these reasons that the prospect of an intensive stay in Italy can be tantamount to an invitation to perfect one's personality in a manner that never ends. A substantial stay in Italy is thus also and unavoidably an archaeological self-excavation, whereby we place our entire lives on the line and in which images, facts, symbols, figures, memories, and fantasies populate our minds in a continuous process of interaction.

FOR SIGMUND FREUD, THE DISCOVERY OF TROY WAS the pinnacle of good fortune, precisely because it was the fulfill-ment of one of Heinrich Schliemann's childhood dreams. For many artists and writers, the first visit to Italy is likewise an experience of immense good fortune, on the one hand because everything is totally new and they can experience it as the fulfill-ment of a childhood dream, and on the other because so many people preceded them in this discovery and left traces of them-selves in the process. Those who come face to face with Italy are confronted with the twofold truth of a historical present and an ever tangible past. In our collective inner world, a mental organ was thus formed, layer by layer, the organ responsible for our 'Italy feeling'. It would probably be too good to be true if that organ one day turns out to be shaped like a boot.

A DANCING FATHER

On the Difference between Black and White

In our present day world as in times gone by it makes a significant difference whether you're born black or white, but conveying that difference in words is a precarious business. The chance of succumbing to dangerous clichés and of stating the obvious is very real, and given that the truth content of such statements can vary considerably according to time, place and specific circumstances, they tend not to offer much by way of useful insight. On the other hand, the fact that the comparison cannot be made on the basis of one single case makes it all the more tricky – a person is born either white or black and has no choice in the matter – unless, of course, just such an instance can be found.

The following small announcement, which appeared in the *New York Times Book Review* on February 18th, 2001, turned out to refer to such a case of black *and* white:

For a book about my father, Anatole Broyard, I would appreciate hearing from anyone with correspondence from him and/or recollections about his life, Bliss Broyard, 96 Schermerhorn Street.

On the surface there's nothing very unusual going on here. A daughter is planning to write a book about her father, Anatole Broyard, who worked for the *New York Times* as an influential and productive literary critic from 1971 to 1989. Literary 'father books' have been a recurrent feature in the English speaking world for several decades. In most instances, the fathers in question are among the Great Writers of our times. Examples include J.D. Salinger, portrayed by his daughter Margaret in *Dream Catcher. A Memoir.* Or *Home Before Dark. A Biographical Memoir by His Daughter* by Susan Cheever written about her father John. Or Greg Bellow's book about his father entitled *Saul Bellow's Heart. A Son's Memoir.* But Anatole Broyard wasn't that great a literary figure, although he was certainly one of the most authoritative American literary reviewers of the 1970s and 80s.

A second category of literary 'father book' exists in which the literary gravity is contributed more by the daughter than the father. This category might include *The Kiss* by Kathryn Harrison, for example, and Germaine Greer's *Daddy, We Hardly Knew You.* These are books in which a daughter-writer tries to come to terms with an important and, for her own life, determinative truth about her father.

It appears that Bliss Broyard's plan to write a book about her father intended from the outset to combine both types of literary 'father book': a book about her father as a public literary figure on the one hand, and on the other a book about the personal secret that he had carried with him all his life, a secret his daughter was determined to unravel once and for all. The secret in question did not only relate to Broyard himself, moreover, it also concerned his two children from his second marriage, and profoundly so.

IT WAS ALREADY CLEAR FROM BLISS BROYARD'S FIRST collection of stories entitled *My Father, Dancing* (1999) that the figure of her father played an important role in her life. Anatole Broyard, who passed away in 1990, is present in the book in a variety of ways, each of the stories being dedicated almost without exception to the relationship between daughters and their fathers. The dedication reads 'In Memory of My Father' and the title story describes the – at first sight – barely fictionalized demise of Anatole Broyard, who died in the hospital from prostate cancer a year after he retired from the *Times*.

Each of the stories in *My Father, Dancing* has a female lead character, varying in age from ten to early twenties. But the key figure in five of the eight stories is a father. In addition to the dying father from the title story, there is a story about a father being caught by his daughter in an adulterous public kiss, for example, while she herself had just spent the night with a casual acquaintance. We also read of a father doing his daughter's homework, a comical account in which his help far from guarantees a good grade. In yet another story, we are told of a father who tries but fails to make a match between his family and a couple with whom he's on friendly terms and who regularly visit for the day on his insistence. In the remaining stories, the young female central figures are likewise obliged to give form to their budding adulthood and hesitant sexual choices in confrontation with imperious and coercive men and boys.

Bliss Broyard describes these human – and mostly male – failings and the unavoidable shortcomings of family life with keenness and without gall. Her portraits of fathers and mothers, daughters and their boyfriends, are sketched with empathy and without redundant commentary. In addition to the usual features of family interaction, her stories also expose an irrational element that leaves sufficient space for the reader to provide his or her own interpretation.

Viewed from a distance, *My Father, Dancing* is the type of literary debut that is usually followed by a second collection or – better still – by a novel in which the author might cast the net a little wider and hope for a more generous catch in terms of themes, characters and narrative lines, thereby further developing her authorial career. All things considered, this is more or less the only thing one can say against Broyard's debut: the father theme is rather limited in scope. Yet this is precisely the theme that was to preoccupy her for years as she researched her next book. The result was *One Drop. My Father's Hidden Life*, a five hundred pager published in 2007. The book's subtitle *A Story of Race and Family Secrets* tantalizingly lifts the veil on Anatole Broyard's secret: he was a black man who had pretended to his dying day that he was white.

ANATOLE PAUL BROYARD WAS BORN IN 1920 IN NEW Orleans, the son of a black father, the carpenter Paul Broyard, and a black mother, Edna Miller. Neither of his parents completed elementary education and Anatole's early years were spent in a poor colored neighborhood in the French speaking part of the city. He later moved with his parents to New York and the primarily black Brooklyn neighborhood where he attended Brooklyn College. In an attempt to escape his black background, and perhaps also his premature marriage to a dark-skinned Puerto Rican woman, he decided to sign up for the American army during World War II *as a white man.* Broyard's facial features were not Negro and his skin color, as is evident from later photos, was remarkably light, more yellowish than black. He succeeded. After officer training, which was restricted to whites, he was given command, ironically enough, of a company of 220 black soldiers and posted to the Far East.

Anatole Broyard was to maintain this ethnic metamorphosis for the rest of his life, not only towards his newspaper colleagues and the outside world, but even towards his own children. In a country as marked by racial and ethnic contrasts as the United States, his masquerade must have been at once both liberating and terrifying. Bliss Broyard provides a detailed and at moments moving sketch of that duality in *One Drop.* For hundreds of pages she excavates her father's family history, exposing once and for all the secret of his ethnic deception in all its complexity, a revelation that for her also must have been an autobiographical journey of discovery.

Bliss Broyard, however, was not the first to get to the bottom of her father's story. A good ten years prior to the publication of her book, a pointed analysis of her father's life story penned by Henry Louis Gates, Jr. appeared in *The New Yorker* in the form of a long essay, later published in a collection under the title 'The Passing of Anatole Broyard'. Gates' analysis is much more painful than that of Broyard's daughter because a certain tone of accusation resounds throughout his portrait, and because his description of the versatile and talented Broyard boils down to the formulation of an ethnic problem: should a black person be free, given the opportunity, to pretend to be white? This question is not only intriguing from the human perspective, it also cries out to be explored in the form of fiction.

When Gates' piece appeared in *The New Yorker*, Philip Roth had just started work on his novel *The Human Stain*, which was to be published in 2000. While Roth publicly denied it more than once – even in the form of a sensational 'open letter to Wikipedia' – many stubbornly insisted that the novelist had based the trans-ethnic central figure of his novel, Coleman Silk, on the life of Anatole Broyard. Whether it's true or not, the fascination of an American novelist for the theme of a voluntary change of race is easy to comprehend. The same fascination applies *a priori* to his daughter, who heard about her father's (and thus her own) ethnic background from her mother only one week before her father died. Anatole Broyard was already in a terminal coma at that time and was no longer able to speak. But he was still able to listen, and the Broyard family – his wife,

son Todd, and daughter Bliss – held conversations at his deathbed about this long concealed subject to make him aware that
his children knew the truth and that they accepted that truth.

IT IS CLEAR FROM THE REST OF HIS LIFE STORY THAT
Anatole Broyard was much more than a 'trans-ethnic *casus*'.
Indeed, as a critic and writer he managed to create tremendous
career possibilities for himself, with his unique, self-chosen, and
fastidiously maintained white identity. After his return from the
war, Broyard settled – as a white man – in New York's Greenwich
Village where he opened an antiquarian bookstore. 'One of the
persistent romances,' he called it, 'like living off the land or sailing around the world.' In the evenings he followed classes at the
New School for Social Research and he started to write.

Towards the end of his life he wrote a small but masterful
book about that period entitled *Kafka Was the Rage. A Greenwich
Village Memoir.* These incomplete memoirs, which were only
published after his death, are quite unequivocal about the fact
that New York's *Village* was just as roaring, hip, and arty in the
1940s and 50s as Paris was in the 20s. In any event, for Broyard
himself it was a liberation, not only on the ethnic level, but also
intellectually, artistically, and especially sexually.

In a compact, satirical, evocative, and seemingly effortless
flowing style, Broyard gives words to his memories, explaining
how all these liberations criss-crossed one another, as it were:
the transition to abstraction in art and literature, the exchange
of prewar domestic emotions for postwar cosmopolitanism, and
the generation-wide discovery of sexuality. As a white man, he
was able to participate in all of this to his heart's content. In

addition to jazz music, books constituted the pulsing heart *par excellence* of this new found 'modern life': Franz Kafka, Wallace Stevens, D.H. Lawrence, and Louis-Ferdinand Céline were his favorites. 'If it hadn't been for books,' he wrote, 'we'd been completely at the mercy of sex.'

Kafka Was the Rage is brim-full of portraits of literary friends, acquaintances, and passers-by, including Delmore Schwartz, Clement Greenberg, Anaïs Nin, W.H. Auden, and Dylan Thomas. In addition, the book is populated by a selection of his New School lecturers (Erich Fromm, Meyer Schapiro), painters and psychiatrists, jazz musicians and Cuban rumba dancers. But the most dominant figure in this *memoir*, perhaps more dominant even than the autobiographical I-figure, is a woman referred to in the book as Sheri Donatti. Artist, protégée of Anaïs Nin, and unsurpassable object of the young Broyard's social and sexual curiosity, she defines his life in those years more than anyone and anything. For that reason the seventeen chapters of *Kafka Was the Rage* are divided into two parts: the first is called 'Sheri', the second 'After Sheri'. Known in real life as Sheri Martinelli, this woman evidently exercised such a power of attraction on authors in particular that the likes of William Gaddis, and later Ezra Pound and Charles Bukowski likewise appeared to have been enthralled by her for years on end. The struggle for her charms Broyard fought out with Gaddis was ultimately immortalized in the latter's 1955 novel *The Recognitions*.

AS A RESULT OF HIS EARLY ARTICLES AND STORIES, published in influential journals such as *Commentary*, *The Partisan Review*, and *Discovery*, and courses in creative writing he started to give, Anatole Broyard acquired a reputation in the course of the 1950s and '60s and – as was long the case with Harold Brodkey – literary expectations were high. Atlantic Monthly Press even paid him a staggering advance of $20,000 for a novel, but the book was never to materialize.

After his marriage to the white and golden-blonde Alexandra Nelson and the birth of their son Todd followed by their daughter Bliss, Broyard spent seven years working as a copywriter for a Manhattan advertising agency. At the same time he started to write literary reviews and essays for the *New York Times*, the paper with which he was later to work as a critic from 1971 until a year before his death in 1990. Those who read his reviews and columns will be unable to miss his intellectual passion and the fact that he was clearly extremely well-read without being bookish. He combined intellectual authority with charm and flair, and was able to make reviews of more popular writers like Judith Krantz or James Michener just as interesting as pieces about the new Vladimir Nabokov or Bernard Malamud. He put together two collections gleaned from his enormous output as an essayist and critic (*Aroused by Books* in 1974 and *Men, Women and Other Anticlimaxes* in 1980), taken together a treasure-trove brimming over with curiosity and the capacity to judge and assess. The posthumous publication of a book about his illness (*Intoxicated by My Illness and Other Writings on Life and Death*) and the aforementioned *Kafka Was the Rage* rounded off his productive and successful career.

And then the truth came to light, a truth that had been gossiped and speculated about among his white contemporaries, but had never acquired a definitive form for lack of clear evidence. The unequivocal truth appeared to be that the white GI, the white career intellectual, the WASP (*White Anglo-Saxon Protestant*) with his house in Connecticut and his vacations on elitist Martha's Vineyard was actually a Creole boy from New Orleans. A black man who had decided at an unguarded moment to spend the rest of his life as a white man and had done so successfully for half a century, until he started to lose control of his secret in the hospital on his seventieth, a week before his death, and so was delivered into the loving grace of his wife and children. Broyard, it appears, didn't have 'a distant black ancestor', but as Gates put it: he might have had one distant white ancestor. His parents, grandparents and great-grandparents were black, pure and simple.

WHAT'S THE DIFFERENCE BETWEEN A BLACK MAN AND a white man? The difference consists in fact not of one but of two human lives, of the sum of the life you lead and the life you don't lead. To make the transition from one identity to the other, Broyard didn't only have to be able to adopt a new and plausible white identity and persevere in it, he also, and more importantly, had to discard his former, black identity and successfully keep it at a distance. He had to hide that cast-off identity as if 'his life depended on it', together with everything and everyone that remembered it or knew about it. Both his daughter's book and Henry Louis Gates' essay provide pithy examples of what that was like, leaving the combined impression of a sort of ethnic paranoia that must have followed Broyard's every footstep, sometimes at very close quarters.

In the eyes of the extremely critical and at times odious Gates, Anatole Broyard denied himself: by abandoning his fellow black men, deceiving his children and hijacking his wife into a secret that she was obliged to guard with him. This is the perspective of a black faultfinder. From my perspective, that of a white man who received his white birthright as self-evident, for whom the color of a person's skin is more of a political and historical issue than an everyday awareness, Anatole Broyard personifies a human, perhaps even superhuman ideal. In postwar America, Broyard's so vigorously coveted white identity was a successful fiction that he managed to live in reality. Perhaps this was why he found it so difficult to steer his creative literary talent in the direction of a novel. It would inevitably have brought him face to face with the fictional boundaries of his own life. Whatever the case, he managed nonetheless to fashion his own fate, and he danced by his own force from one race to another. Anatole Broyard was the living difference between a black man and a white man.

THE LATERVEER BOX

Your Own Family and Other People's

Aunt Laura Beer née Benjamin wasn't the type you wanted to get into an argument with. In a desk portrait she had had taken of herself at photographers Wegner & Mottu on Amsterdam's fashionable Kalverstraat ('over den Heyligenweg D.26') she sits and stares uncompromisingly into the camera. Under her left elbow, which is resting firmly on an occasional table, a hardcover book is clearly visible and with a magnifying glass it's just possible to distinguish the writing on its spine: 'Volume I'. She's wearing her hair George Sand style and the sleeves of her velvet jacket – decorative buttons and stitching in abundance – are edged with fur. Below the jacket her enormous broad skirt billows tremendously, as if Aunt Laura is in danger of exploding from impatience at any minute. Judging by the print technique, the photograph was probably taken around 1860. The addition of the so-called 'Neighborhood Letter D' to the house number means it can't have been taken before 1851.

And what about the vaguely androgynous Dina Benjamin? Her gentle, ethereal air is clear to see in a portrait taken in 1906 in the studios of Koene & Büttinghausen, on the corner of the Herengracht and the Leliegracht. The building can still be recognized from the remarkable glass roof on the Leliegracht side, which marks the place where the studio once was. Dina lost her husband Salomon (Sally) Cohen a few years earlier, after a marriage that lasted thirty-two years. Perhaps that explains the empty, compassionate look on her face, although it didn't stop her from dressing up for the occasion in a dazzlingly white dress with a high embroidered collar. There's something priestly about her, especially with the collar in combination with the combed back hair, leading one to hesitate between male and female.

But if you really want to see at a glance what life does to a person's looks then you should place two portraits of Clara Benjamin, married name Clara Würbelduer, side by side. The first was taken in her home in Wiesbaden in the 1880s at the Rumbler-Wirbelauer studio on Rheinstraße 15, opposite the station. According to the internet it's presently the address of the tourist information office, although it's easy to guess that the original building has probably been replaced since then by something new. The first photo was taken early in her marriage, her hair tied up and crowned with a fancy pin. She's flanked by her two children, one of them still a baby of less than a year old, the other a boy of three, judging by appearances. Clara peers at the lens with a softhearted, emotional look in her eyes. The second photo was taken almost thirty years later, a couple of streets away at the Kauer & Schröder studio on Taunusstraße 17. Here we see Clara as a prosperous but seasoned woman. Her left hand is resting tensely and unnaturally on a book lying open on a pedestal. In contrast to her tightly laced-up torso, her dark floral dress hangs loosely over her hips in extra wide folds. Her eyes are sunken, inclining one to wonder with some apprehension what might have happened to the children who no longer accompany her.

The oldest of the two children was called Fritz, and Clara's husband was Louis Würbelduer. In 1897, the then roughly twelve-year-old Fritz also joined his father on a visit to the photographer's studio, the same Rumbler-Wirbelauer studio that had since relocated to Wilhelmstraße 14 in Wiesbaden. The boy is standing upright in his obligatory sailor suit and his father is at his side on an ottoman wearing a formal jacket with light summer pants. For the occasion of this immortalization of himself and his oldest son, he's curled his moustache in such a way that it sticks out a distance on either side of his face. The rear of the print states '*Die Platte bleibt aufbewahrt* – The plate is being preserved', next to a list of all the prizes Rumbler studio had bagged down through the years, with the title 'Photographers to the Court of the Greek Royal Family' as its biggest claim to fame. But who can say what happened to the young Fritz Würbelduer after the photo was taken. The date alone is enough to elicit an involuntary shiver, three years before the turn of the century. In 1914, Fritz would have been twenty-nine or thereabouts, and in 1933 forty-eight, to name a couple of dates that would not have been entirely insignificant for a Jewish family from Wiesbaden.

Fritz Würbelduer's trail dries up at this point, although he might be present on the far left of a so-called 'collodion wet plate' from around 1920. The razor sharp print depicts an entire family, thirteen people in total, gathered around a couple of tables with wine and appetizers. But it might also be his younger brother, blossomed in the meantime into a well-groomed young gentleman in a suit with a stand-up collar and spotless cuffs. A respectable young woman is sitting at his side, leaning forward slightly and looking into the camera with a serious expression on her face. There's little in terms of festiveness to be detected in the photograph; rather reticence and a hint of mystery seem to dominate, forcing one to guess whether this reunited family had something to celebrate or lament. Tacked to the side of a display cabinet to the right at the back of the room one can just make out a portrait of Johann Sebastian Bach, and as I carefully examine this photo, the opening words of Cantata BWV 26 resound in my head as a sort of caption: *'Ach wie flüchtig, ach wie nichtig ist der Menschen Leben* – Ah, how fleeting, ah how insignificant is the life of mankind.'

MANY YEARS AGO, MY FATHER MET A RETIRED POLICE spokesman and journalist by the name of Nico Laterveer at the Nieuwspoort Press Centre in The Hague. The man told him he had a box at home full of old photos of the Asschers, which he had acquired from the estate of a housekeeper who had once worked for the family. Such information fires the imagination, of course, and shortly after the meeting my father headed to

Voorschoten and the Laterveer residence to pick up the box. Once home he sifted through the entire pile, but there was no trace of an Asscher. He asked around, gave the box to members of another Asscher family when the opportunity arose, but no one managed to identify a single member of the Asscher family in the multitude of (group) portraits, snapshots and desk photos.

The box was alive with names that a former – or perhaps the original – owner had added obligingly by hand to the back of each photo: Uncle Albert Benjamin, Leo Löwenblum, Louise Beer, Mr De Vries, Mrs De Vries, Uncle Moritz Benjamin, Leon Wertheim, Aunt Jülchen Latz née Benjamin, Hedwig Hirschland, Ida Beer, Uncle Bloemendal, Samson Seligmann, Fredrik Wertheim. But no Asschers. The earliest photos dated from around 1860, the most recent from around 1920. Some were taken in Germany – Wiesbaden, Cologne, Cottbus, Essen, Bonn, Düsseldorf, Kassel, Karlsbad, Munich – others in the Netherlands – from Maastricht to Wageningen and from Almelo to Amsterdam – and a few in Paris, Vienna, and Marienbad. There were cheap holiday snaps among them from a windy day at the beach, but also rare albumenized salt prints from the early years of photography. But again, there was no trace of an Asscher family connection.

I INHERITED THE 'LATERVEER BOX', AS THE CARDBOARD thing came to be known, from my father and it's now stored away with my other archive stuff. My own investigations likewise failed to make a family connection, but strange as it may seem, the box has become part of the family nonetheless. It was an abandoned family and I took it in, for better or for worse, as if these uncles and aunts, great-grandparents, second cousins and nieces once removed were and are my own flesh and blood. For what does 'family' mean? When you're young, family is the lively spectacle on birthdays and other festivities, the presents, the arguments, the weddings, the births. But as the years pass, family becomes a web of stories and secrets, irretrievable histories and inherited memories, which together constitute a novel that can never be completed. And what is the difference after the passage of one and a half centuries between a photo of your own great-grandfather whom you never met and a photo of someone else's great-grandfather, on the back of which someone has written with love: 'León Wertheim, husband of Augusta Wertheim-Gans'. Surrounded by photos of his loved ones and descendents, such a person slowly but surely becomes your own kin, just as a cherished character from a novel can become part of your personal emotional community.

Aunt Laura Beer, Clara and Dina Benjamin, Louis and Fritz Würbelduer have entered the room unnoticed and quietly taken their place in the group portrait of my own family history. They stand in their midst as if they could start a conversation with any of the others at the drop of a hat. And when I look at these familiar strangers I have the feeling I could tell you all sorts of details about them. But silence is better, because I would doubtless draw the irrevocable ire of aunt Laura on my head. Her reputation reverberates across the generations, and I close the 'Laterveer Box' as if I'm tucking my own past history in for the night. Will some future descendant one day discover the missing link that in one or another surprising way connects these distant relatives to me?

NOT THE BARS BUT THE DOOR

Writing in a Prison Cell and in a Study

For the evening of November 27th, 1909, Marcel Proust had invited ten or so of his closest friends to join him for a visit to the theater and a performance of Georges Feydeau's new comedy *Le Circuit*. Proust had reserved no fewer than three boxes for his sizeable party of companions at the Parisian *Théâtre des Variétés*, and after the show he dined at length with his friends at restaurant *Chez Larue* on the *Place de la Madeleine*.

The grandiosity of Proust's plan was not inspired by the importance of the theater première with which the evening's program was to commence. *Le Circuit* is more of an entertaining comedy of manners than a theatrical literary masterpiece, situated in the world of the automobile, a relatively recent invention in those days that brought the classes closer together and thereby facilitated amorous complications. Will the garage owner's niece run off with the rich industrialist, or will she stay faithful to the young car mechanic Étienne? *That is the question.*

The idea behind Proust's desire to celebrate this particular Saturday evening with his friends was of a different order, although it was not mentioned in the course of the festivities. Consciously or unconsciously, Proust set out to mark the date in question as a historical moment, the moment at which he planned to withdraw completely from the world and shut himself away in order to devote the rest of his time, concentration, and talent to writing what was to become his great, all-embracing novel *À la recherche du temps perdu.* Everything had been made ready for this '*rite de passage*'; only a demarcation was necessary between the past of yesterday and the future that was to begin the following morning. For the remaining thirteen years of his life, Marcel Proust retired to a series of addresses, lodging in rooms with cork covered walls to keep out the noise of the world. He was to live an inverted life, working through the night, and if not sleeping during the day, then resting in solitary timidity. November 27th, 1909, honored with good reason by French Proust expert Alain Buisine with a 231-page monograph, formed the symbolic threshold of his departure. Roland Barthes speaks of that moment in the writer's life as an '*entrer dans un livre* – entering into a book', a formula with a monastic resonance.

Those visiting the Parisian Musée Carnavalet's reconstruction of Proust's tiny bedroom-cum-study, based on his lodgings in Boulevard Haussmann 102, might even go a step further. Further, I mean, than the comparison with the ever voluntary choice of a life in a monastic cell. The comparison with imprisonment also presents itself; the author as prisoner of the work to which he is destined, the work he is unable to escape; serving time as a self-imposed punishment until the work is completed. As far as Proust and his *Recherche* were concerned this was nothing short of a life sentence.

Such a comparison might sound bizarre at first and perhaps slightly decadent, but the question – posed not in legal but in literary terms – remains: what precisely is the difference between 'voluntary' confinement and involuntary confinement? In other words: what is the difference for a writer between a prison cell and a study? The answer to this question is important among other things for its inevitable follow-up question: is there such a thing as prison literature, and if there is how should it be defined?

IN MY ENDEAVOR TO ANSWER THESE QUESTIONS I WILL explore primarily Western European literary history from the French Revolution to the Second World War, the one and a half centuries between 1789 and 1945. A long literary procession precedes this period, not only of those imprisoned by the courts, but also ecclesial, political, and even scientific martyrs, many of whom made a contribution to civilization from a prison cell. But the experience of long periods of solitary confinement as a socially imposed punishment is typically associated with the prison reforms initiated in the last quarter of the eighteenth century that went hand in hand with the emergence of urban industrialized society. And in the period since 1945, phenomena such as rehabilitation, probationary release, and detention guidance have evolved, together with a broadly greater emphasis on inmate well-being.

My geographical limitations are also justifiable. Outside Europe, North American prison literature has been more or less unique in its inexhaustible contribution to the expansion of the genre, with its tradition of nineteenth-century 'slave narratives' and twentieth-century 'death row' testimonies.

Anyone taking a closer look at Western European prison literature from Romanticism to the Second World War will observe a recurrent series of universal themes, irrespective of whether the author was left to rot in a 1820s Austrian dungeon, confined to a Victorian prison cell in London, or held by the Gestapo during the Second World War. In this sense, prison literature would appear to detach itself to a degree from the history of literature that was developing in freedom outside the prison gates. One can presume that this has to do with the extreme material limitations and intellectual isolation that hold sway when writing in a prison cell. Those who are forced to confront the fundamental humanity of surviving in solitude day after day will also, and inevitably, be confronted with timeless questions and timeless answers.

This thematic unity is clearly observable in the public protest Oscar Wilde registered against the treatment he received in prison. After his release in 1897 from Reading Prison, where he had served the greater part of a sentence handed down for 'gross indecency' (i.e. having sex with young men), he published a call for the reform of the Victorian punitive system on two levels. Detailed in a letter to the *Daily Chronicle* of March 24th, 1898, the two levels addressed the systematic physical and mental suffering imposed on prisoners in English prisons. According to Wilde, physical suffering consisted primarily of hunger, sleep deprivation, and sickness. Mental suffering, which he believed could be easily alleviated, had to do with the absence of quality reading material in prison and with the lack of opportunity for visits and other human contact.

The same points of critique might also have been applied to a prison experience from the beginning of the nineteenth century, and in essence could have been introduced – at least in most European countries – against the prison conditions that dominated until shortly after the Second World War. In other words, conditions in European prisons between the beginning of the nineteenth century and the middle of the twentieth are sufficiently comparable to justify an endeavor to establish connections between the experience of imprisonment and its potential literary yield. The American literary theorist W.B. Carnochan rightly speaks of 'imaginative continuities' in the history of prison literature that deserve preference above 'historical discontinuities'.

IF ONE FOCUSES MORE CLOSELY ON THE PHENOMENON of prison literature, a term one would seek in vain in the majority of handbooks of literary theory, it is possible to distinguish three manifestations thereof. But before we explore these three categories and illustrate them with examples, we first need to establish what we mean by the concept 'prison'.

An entire literature has emerged in the twentieth century written by victims of persecution, many of whom have shared time with many other companions in adversity in a concentration camp or an extermination camp. Their memories, written down by survivors, are often referred to with the term '(prison) camp literature'. Books of this sort, written for the most part by Jewish writers of varying nationalities such as Primo Levi, Gerhard Durlacher, and André Schwarz-Bart, are certainly related to the phenomenon of prison literature, but at the same time they are clearly different. The camps to which they refer were places in which masses of people were put to work or exterminated on an industrial scale, while a prison cell is a place of solitary confinement, occasionally with one or two fellow prisoners, but mostly alone. This is a crucial difference from the perspective of human experience, a difference deftly expressed in the definition the Russian poet Joseph Brodsky once gave to a prison: 'A lack of space, counterbalanced by a surplus of time.'

In addition, and as a result of wars, political repression, poverty, and religious intolerance – especially in the twentieth century – a literature of exile has emerged, written by authors who were forced to produce their work, often initially in social isolation, from a country that was not their own. Here too we can observe a not insignificant element of constraint, but it is not the constraint of being literally locked up in a room, being forced to exist within four walls, with no opportunity for escape. Exiles do not experience confinement in the literal sense of the term.

Parallels can also be drawn between prison literature and the literature written in psychiatric institutions, monastery cells, boarding schools, sanatoria, for example, or other sometimes extreme forms of isolation. As far as I am concerned, thematic parallels can be drawn to the extent that such circumstances are comparable with life in a prison cell. But in the strict sense, the combined experience of punishment, confinement, and solitude applies only to prisons and I will thus limit my focus to the literature to which they give rise, subdivided, as noted above, into three categories.

THE PUREST SORT OF PRISON LITERATURE, AND ALSO the sort people tend to think about first when they hear the expression, is the literary work written by a person from a situation of imprisonment. The work in question can be a reconstruction of or a reflection on the person's vicissitudes, as in the posthumously published *De Profundis* by Oscar Wilde, *Notre-Dame-des-Fleurs* (1944) by the literary thief Jean Genet, or *Soul on Ice* (1968) by the black American essayist Eldridge Cleaver, who had been imprisoned for rape. It might also be a series of poems inspired by existence within the four walls of a cell, such as the *Moabiter Sonette* by Albrecht Haushofer and the *Poèmes de Fresnes* by Robert Brasillach, both written in the more or less inescapable expectation of impending execution. Reference can also be made to the sonnet cycle *In Excelsis* written from prison by Lord Alfred Douglas, the title a tribute to his former friend Oscar Wilde. It goes without saying that the work in question need not have to do with the condition of incarceration as such, at least not directly. If you are unaware that the Marquis de Sade's libertine novel *Justine* (1787) was written in prison, you will never be able to guess on the basis of the book's contents alone.

The number of criminals who only started to write after they landed in prison is positively legion and they are perhaps better designated literary criminals rather than imprisoned writers. This can be said of Jean Genet, for example, but also for Eldridge Cleaver, aggressive and talented in equal measure, who would not have landed in prison without his crimes, would not have enjoyed much of an education without his repeated periods of incarceration, and would certainly not have started to write letters and essays without imprisonment and education. Be that as it may, countless prisoners have written letters from prison. In some instances – as in the case of Oscar Wilde's *De Profundis* – the letters in question are included as part of their literary oeuvre. But given that the limits of what we consider to be a literary text and the designation of the circumstances under which a letter can also serve as a literary work are not issues that pertain specifically to the topic of prison literature, I will not rehearse them further here, in spite of their potential importance.

The second category of prison literature relates to the work produced by writers after their release, in which they report on the incarceration they have undergone. A celebrated example of this category dating from the nineteenth century is Silvio Pellico's *Le mie prigioni*, a book of memoirs published in 1832 after a total of almost ten years in Austrian prisons paying the price for his casual association with the movement that tried to resist Austria's rule over the Northern Italian states. The South African born poet, writer, and painter Breyten Breytenbach, who was imprisoned by the apartheid regime between 1975 and 1982, offers a modern example of this retrospective, auto-biographical prison literature with his *The True Confessions of an Albino Terrorist* (1983).

The third manifestation of prison literature is the fictional work in which the experience of incarceration plays a prominent role, such as Lord Byron's narrative poem *The Prisoner of Chillon* (1816) or Stendhal's novel *La Chartreuse de Parme* (1839). Such fiction is sometimes inspired by the author's own memories of a period in prison, as is the case with Arthur Koestler's *Darkness at Noon* (1940) or the Peruvian José Maria Arguedas' *El Sexto* (1961). Other examples are – as far as I am aware – entirely fictional, like Albert Camus' *L'étranger* (1942), John Banville's *The Book of Evidence* (1989) or A.F.Th. van der Heijden's *Het schervengericht – Ostracism* (2007). Reference can be made in terms of Dutch poetry to Jan Campert's ballad *De achttien doden – The Eighteen Dead*, which bases its theme on reports about the execution by the Nazis of a group of Dutch resistance fighters in 1941.

These are the three basic forms of prison literature: work written from a prison cell, work written after a period of incarceration, and work in which imprisonment – sometimes based on the author's personal experience, sometimes not – has a role to play in a fictional context. What can we learn from this subdivision?

This subdivision teaches us virtually nothing about the formal aspect of prison literature. The examples to which I've referred include prose and poetry, autobiography and fiction. The suggestion that prison literature can be designated a literary genre or subgenre is thus clearly open to question. A dilemma of this sort inevitably draws us back to the primordial question of literary theory over which Aristotle himself agonized: in which cases does it make sense to ascribe certain types of writing to a distinct genre. The same question can be asked with respect to the location in which a work takes place or where it was written. Thomas Mann (*Der Zauberberg* – *The Magic Mountain*), David Vogel (*In the Sanatorium*) and Salvatore Satta (*La veranda*), for example, all wrote novels that take place in a sanatorium. A comparison of the three books would certainly be an interesting endeavor, but should it lead us to proclaim the existence of a new genre of 'sanatorium literature'? The fact that all three novels focus on the 'existential experience' of the sanatorium patient as a particularization of the human condition might argue in favor of such a proclamation. On the other hand, what does the establishment of a (sub)genre add to our capacity to make meaningful comparative statements about novels that happen to be situated in a sanatorium?

In their manual *Inleiding in de literatuurwetenschap* – *Introduction to Literary Theory*, J. Van Luxemburg, M. Bal and W.G. Weststeijn appear to claim that the more books written about a given topic – they refer to 'the death of a father' by way of example – the more reason there is to consider defining a genre. But instead of circumscribing prison literature and forcing it to fit within the limits of an aspect of *form*, namely subject matter, as a distinct genre, I am more inclined – here at least – to take a closer look at the three types of prison literature in terms of their *content*.

THE FIRST THING TO OBSERVE IS THAT PRISON LITERA-ture covers an extremely broad spectrum. One extreme is formed by texts that were written in the immediate context of imprisonment, often under difficult and limiting circumstances. Oscar Wilde's well-intentioned prison governor Major Nelson gave him a copybook and blue-lined folio sheets to allow him to write with at least a semblance of normality, but Albrecht Haushofer – held in a Gestapo prison in Berlin under suspicion of involvement in the attack on Adolf Hitler on July 20th, 1944 – was forced to scribble his eighty sonnets on the front and back of five scraps of paper. And Lord Alfred Douglas, imprisoned for five months in Wormwood Scrubs in 1923-1924 for insulting Winston Churchill, wasn't even allowed to take the manuscript of the cycle of poems he had composed in his cell with him when he was set free. The prison authorities insisted that the document was prison property and thus belonged to the crown. According to British archive legislation it will only be released in 2043! Fortunately Douglas took the trouble to memorize the seventeen sonnets and was able to reconstruct the entire manuscript when he arrived home. As a result, it was published in book form in 1924.

The second category of prison literature, work written after release, also includes material in which the extreme circumstances of incarceration feature prominently, especially, for example, where the trauma of imprisonment continues to govern the life of the ex-detainee. Such documents likewise contain extremely realistic descriptions of the circumstances under which the writers endeavored to pen their thoughts. Silvio Pellico states that he wrote messages to his fellow prisoners in his own blood, greatly endangering himself, the receiver, and last but by no means least the prison guard found willing to smuggle them from one cell to another.

At the other extreme of the spectrum we encounter the work of novelists who include the experience of imprisonment among the vicissitudes faced by a fictional character. Take Fabrizio del Dongo, for example, the nobleman in the *Chartreuse de Parme*, who Stendhal locates in a cell in Parma's highest tower. From his place of isolation, Fabrizio maintains an impossible love affair – nourished by exchanged glances and secret signs – with a woman who appears every now and then on her balcony opposite the prison tower, the daughter of the prison governor.

On closer inspection, however, the apparent antithesis between extreme realism and quasi-decadent romanticism in the articulation and portrayal of prison experience teaches us that there is more to be said for a flowing transition than a sharp contrast. In some instances, what appear to be extremes have much in common. While it's true that Stendhal, for example, colored his prison scenes with the shades of adventure and passion characteristic of an 1830s Romantic, the author confesses nevertheless in both the novel itself and in his letters, that he was indebted for certain details to the descriptions Silvio Pellico provided in *Le mie prigioni* of his incarceration in a series of prison cells.

A flowing transition is also evident in the opposite direction when we realize that the so-called realistic descriptions of prison experience are rarely if ever as realistic as their authors would have us believe. This is already the case *a priori*, since the creative hand of a writer always constructs an experience, one that he or she is undergoing at the time of writing or one he or she has already experienced. And as soon as an experience is consigned to paper it ceases to be a reality and the experience that has been written down becomes a new *literary* reality. It is hardly surprising therefore that writers who begin their prison memoirs with a declaration insisting that what follows is the plain and unadorned truth, consciously or unconsciously deviate, adorn and vary, if only to give their descriptions a little more narrative than a bare summary of observed facts would have to offer. Silvio Pellico is a case in point. At the end of chapter LXXXI of his memoirs, he describes an emotional moment at the deathbed of a very elderly prison guard, Schiller by name, who had become a cherished friend during his years of incarceration in Spielberg Castle. The moment, complete with inconsolable foster daughter for whom the dying man slips a silver ring from his finger before closing his eyes for eternity, cannot have been witnessed by Pellico in person because he was locked up in an underground dungeon at the time.

IN SHORT, EVEN A CURSORY ANALYSIS OF THE THREE apparently so distinct categories of prison literature reveals that, as is often the case, appearances can be deceptive. Prison literature's realism supposedly evident in the first two categories isn't – by a long shot – a carbon copy of reality, and the romanticism of prison literature exemplified in the third category often appears to be rooted in its turn in reality as experienced by the author or borrowed from the first hand descriptions of someone who lived through such incarceration. This leads us to the bothersome possibility – bothersome because it sows doubt with respect to an already raised expectation – that prison literature as a distinct genre does not exist, and that the prison documents belonging to the first two categories cannot even be distinguished with clarity in terms of content from documents that stem from other toilsome or solitary circumstances. If this is so, then the condition of the imprisoned writer may only differ by degrees and not fundamentally from the imprisonment to which every writer ultimately submits, the voluntary isolation needed and the solitariness that is essential to every concentrated literary endeavor. Is there no difference after all between a prison cell and a writer's study?

THE FRENCH LITERARY THEORIST AND SEMIOTICIAN Roland Barthes has made a detailed study of the circumstances in which a writer comes to write a literary work. In a course of lectures given during the academic year 1979-1980 at the Collège de France under the title *La préparation du roman – The Preparation of the Novel*, he explores the circumstances of writing down to the last detail. In addition to seclusion, preparatory reading, a methodical plan, perseverance etc., he states at a given moment: '*Écrire a besoin de clandestinité*'. Writers, according to Barthes, need to work in hiding, as it were, until their work is finished and they can return to the world. In Barthes' methodological portrait of a fictional writer, a solitary, self-concealing heroism comes to the fore that gradually acquires the features of martyrdom. In one of his last lectures, Barthes describes the emergence of a literary work from these impossible, solitary, and oppressive circumstances as '*le miracle de la chambre*'. The question thus arises: does this allow us to draw a parallel between the study of one author and the prison cell of another? 'Le miracle de la cellule' as the perverse pinnacle of a literary prison experience?

This is precisely what the Australian writer Tony Perrottet does in an article published in the *New York Times*. The title of the piece already says enough and immediately elicits – for me at least – the strongest possible resistance: 'Why Writers Belong Behind Bars'. Perrottet's point is that down through the centuries the best writers have consistently sought or created circumstances for their work that resembled those of a prison. Imprisonment for Perrottet is a tried and tested means for avoiding distraction and disciplining one's concentration and zest for work. Quoting the French writer Colette, he states: 'A prison cell is an ideal place to work.'

But Perrottet ultimately over shoots the mark with his idealization of the prison cell as the perfect writer's study, led astray no doubt by his heroes Casanova and Sade. He extols the solitary silence, the untroubled concentration of a room that protects the writer from the racket of worldly concerns, but in my view he overlooks *one* cardinal feature: he pays insufficient attention to the fact that the imprisoned writer is robbed of a say concerning his or her isolation on account of the cell door that is locked from outside.

Ironically enough, it is precisely a novel that supplies the ideal passage to illustrate this point and to introduce the desired delimitation between documents written in prison and works that are created in an ordinary study. At the beginning of chapter 44 of Stendhal's 1830 novel *Le rouge et le noir* – *The Red and the Black*, Julien Sorel laments in his cell prior to his execution: 'The worst of being in prison [...] is not being able to lock one's own door.' This in my opinion is the most compact summary of the difference – in principle, not in degrees - between the free and the imprisoned writer. Prison literature is thus not typified by lonely isolation as such. Imprisoned writers are indeed cut off, behind bars, but this is a condition that can be compared in essence with the isolation sought by every writer. Imprisoned writers' real lack of freedom is located in a lack of power over their isolation. It's not about the bars, it's about the door.

THIS BRINGS US BACK TO MARCEL PROUST'S INSULATED room so splendidly reconstructed in the Musée Carnavalet. The writer first withdrew from the world into his room, then withdrew from his room, as it were, by staying in bed, and while in bed withdrew even further by living exclusively in the past. This threefold withdrawal derived its value from the fact that Proust was free at every moment to reverse each step, a freedom he refused to exercise as much as he could from November 27th, 1909, onwards. To some degree, every writer is a prisoner to his writing, but only free writers have the simultaneous good fortune of being their own prison guard.

THE VILLAGE AND THE WORLD

On Het uur van de rebellen – The Rebels' Hour by Lieve Joris

ertain pieces of advice, spoken or penned by great writers and intended to set the authors of the next generation on the right path, are often quoted. Maxim Gorky for example, advised the young Isaac Babel to 'get out into the world' and Stéphane Mallarmé recommended that his disciple Paul Valéry seek solitude at the beginning of his career as a poet: 'Quant à des conseils, seul en donne la solitude.' During an evening dealing with wartime press coverage, I once heard the noted CNN journalist Peter Arnett preach his personal professional creed to his Dutch colleague Raymond van den Boogaard: 'Save your ass and get the story back.'

Useful pieces of advice, perhaps, but not exactly mutually inclusive. Still, Lieve Joris has so far succeeded by and large to observe all three of these recommendations in her work. She has been 'into the world', in the Arabic world, in Congo, in Hungary, in Egypt, in Syria, in Mali. In each instance, she has succeeded in returning safely and always with a story under her belt. She has also succeeded in putting her story onto paper in the solitude of her study, from her debut *De Golf* – *The Gulf*, now twenty years ago, to her 2008 book *Het uur van de rebellen* – *The Rebels' Hour* and beyond. Anyone inclined to explore her output over the last two decades, however, will quickly realize that as a writer she has completely ignored one well-known piece of authorial advice, and perhaps the most famous recommendation of all. It was Leo Tolstoy's, who said: 'If you want to deal with universal themes, write about your own village.'

Lieve Joris' own village is Neerpelt, a dusty, secluded little town in Belgian Limburg, criss-crossed by the Bocholt-Herentals canal and the river Dommel, and a location that has gone almost completely unmentioned in the dozen or so books she has published to date. One would almost be tempted to say that the author has consciously and with immense tenacity turned Tolstoy's advice on its head: 'If you want to deal with universal themes, write about *someone else's* village.'

The official website of the municipality of Neerpelt refers to the town's motto as 'convivial, dynamic, green and young', not exactly the environment Lieve Joris has sought out by preference as the location of two decades of writing. It would be hard to describe Damascus under the watchful eye of the secret police as 'convivial', 'dynamic' would be something of an understatement when referring to years of African war, if there's anything 'green' in the Arab Gulf States it's the oil revenue dollars, and the velvet revolution in Hungary was anything but 'young'.

Lieve Joris' personal quest through decades of writing and several books has been the search for universal themes as they manifest themselves in a variety of different cities, regions, and countries. Tourists tend to pass over such themes, literally, in their airplanes, heading towards the next holiday destination. Even the serious traveler risks missing them, since reality is, was, and always will be a primordial forest of which only the façade is visible. What then should a writer do? In the last analysis, it's still someone else's village. You're not sure of your way at the start, the unwritten rules remain hidden, and the village's history is not part of you. How can you write both personally and universally on a world that isn't yours?

I believe it's on this point that Lieve Joris substantiates her qualities as a writer, and her book *Het uur van de rebellen – The Rebels' Hour* is an excellent example of her craftsmanship in this regard. The following statement appears at the beginning of the book by way of explanation: 'This book is based on existing characters, situations, and places, without matching them completely.' Such a phrase would not be out of place at the beginning of a literary novel, and is in fact to be found in many. Take the statement from the opening pages of Michael Ondaatje's *The English Patient,* for example: 'While some of the characters who appear in this book are based on historical figures and while many of the areas described [...] exist, it is important to stress that this story is a fiction [...].' The boundary between

Lieve Joris' methodological explanation and that of Michael Ondaatje would appear – in principle – to reflect the difference between non-fiction and fiction, but in fact it's so narrow that the reader has to be careful not to overlook it, because there is another important difference at stake.

HET UUR VAN DE REBELLEN – THE REBELS' HOUR describes the fortunes of a young soldier named Assani who comes from the eastern part of the immeasurable Congo, the Central African region bordering Rwanda and Burundi. This is where he was born, half orphaned, on February 2nd, 1967. His country's capital is Kinshasa, roughly 1000 miles to the west; spelled out in words: one thousand miles. By European standards it's incomprehensible. It's almost like being born in Neerpelt and having your country's government in the Ukrainian capital Kiev.

Assani is African, his nationality Congolese, but in terms of ethnic background he is a Tutsi, and his people, to complicate matters further, are from the Mulenge. Half a life story is hidden in this set of identities, the other half is thrust upon him by history, a history of dictatorship, corruption, civil war, oppression, tribal feuds, rebellions, genocide, three African wars, poverty, hunger, and an uncurbed supply of armaments.

The major difference between the work of Lieve Joris and the work of those who write fiction based on historical material is that history in *Het uur van de rebellen* is still far from being history. Rather it is current affairs, hot off the press. The main character of this book is still not sure of his life. His existence is one of extremes, from fugitive rebel to senior officer in the

Congolese army. Even after the much-praised democratic elections in his country, the first in forty years, the actual men and women that are given a face for us along with Assani, are still prey to the most immense political and human uncertainty. The way in which Lieve Joris effectively and authentically presents the main character of her book, based on years of meetings and conversations and complete with a world of memories, thoughts, and fears, goes far beyond the convention among fiction writers to briefly explore the locations they plan to employ in their novels. What Lieve Joris does is not simply *field research*, it is literary vivisection on history as it is being made.

The result of this vivisection – and this is what makes her relationship with writers of literary fiction so interesting – is put together with the most literary of means: characters, diverse narrative perspectives, flashbacks and flash forwards, narrated time passing in such a way that the development of the various characters is made both visible and tangible. To use a variant of the CNN motto: *Het uur van de rebellen* is 'Literature as it happens.'

The above-mentioned Peter Arnett, who witnessed wars and conflicts from Vietnam to the first Gulf War as the eyes and ears of the world for no less than 35 years, had something else to say during his conversation with Raymond van den Boogaard in Amsterdam. Arnett made a distinction between wars that interested him and wars that didn't, and as a salient example of an unimportant war he made reference to what he termed the one between the 'the Hutsis and the Tutsis'. Coming from him, it sounded like a reference to a comic movie: 'The Hutsis and the Tutsis.' The conversation took place in Amsterdam on

April 27th, 1994. At that very moment – beginning on April 6th to be precise – one of the most brutal genocides in twentieth century world history was in full swing. In little more than three months, roughly 800,000 Tutsis were murdered by Hutu militia, with their bare hands, with clubs and machetes, sometimes up to 10,000 on a single day. The CNN star reporter, awarded the 1966 Pulitzer Prize for his coverage of Vietnam, found it an unimportant war.

Against the background of this unfortunately not unique western disinterest when it comes to the long-running humanitarian and political tragedy of Central Africa, Lieve Joris' *Het uur van de rebellen* – *The Rebels' Hour* is an all the more valuable book, because it interweaves this tragedy with the cheerless, anxious, moving story of the life of one single human being in his own complex and threatening environment. The author thus succeeds in making the drama of an incomprehensible historical reality, which is still ongoing, comprehensible in each of the 256 pages of her book.

If a non-fiction writer, bursting with empathy and narrative vigor, is capable of such a feat, then we must look for a completely different interpretation of Tolstoy's recommendation that authors ought to write about their own village if we want to find a satisfactory explanation for the enormous impression this book leaves with the reader. Indeed, perhaps Lieve Joris has been observing Tolstoy's advice to perfection all these years and it may well be that the universal and personal energy found in her books is encapsulated in this very fact. The only thing you need to understand, however, is that Lieve Joris considers half the world to be her village.

ERNEST DOWSON AND FRANCIS DONNE

What It's Like to Die

Can the literary description of someone's deathbed ever do justice to a person's fight for life in the last few hours of their earthly existence? There are many death scenes in world literature that are famous for their seemingly flawless fidelity to the indescribable reality of a person's last moments. Take Tolstoy's *The Death of Ivan Ilych*, for example, or the glorious description of the death of Don Fabrizio in Giuseppe Tomasi di Lampedusa's *Il Gattopardo – The Leopard*. A less well known writer from the English nineteenth-century *fin de siècle* by the name of Ernest Dowson can, in my opinion, rightly claim to have written a story about the process of dying that can survive comparison with the real thing. But then Dowson had the questionable advantage of having been able to observe death at very close quarters, even, indeed, from the inside out.

Ernest Dowson lived a short life from 1867 to 1900. And if we are to believe the personal memories of R. Thurston Hopkins about this English poet, translator, and prose writer published under the title *A London Phantom*, Dowson during the final years of his life never went out without a revolver in his pocket. It wasn't a brazenly large weapon – such would have been out of character – rather it was a small, slender pocket gun with silver fittings, which he was proud to pass round in writers' cafés and bars for those who were interested in taking a closer look. Given the fact that Dowson didn't have the money in those days to buy such an object, it's probable that he won the far from innocent toy in a bet or a game of cards. Be that as it may, the image of a young poet with a revolver is certainly pregnant with symbolic significance, and in Ernest Dowson's case all the more so since fate had seen to it that he was born with a bullet in his chest in the form of a predisposition for tuberculosis, the sickness that was to govern his life and determine its end at the age of thirty-two. Whether it was due to predestination or the general inclination to dissolution characteristic of England's overripe *fin de siècle* literary climate, the fact remains that Dowson's work is marked by death, existential ennui, and an all-nourishing pessimism. In spite of this, his poems, stories, and novels are far from dreary. His style is too clear, his language too melodious, and his tone too much enamored for dreariness. 'There are some miseries,' says a character in one of his stories, 'that are like happiness.' And Dowson's awareness of the general futility of things, a nihilistic approach to life influenced by his reading of Schopenhauer, did not prevent him from producing a very respectable volume of work in his otherwise short life.

DOWSON'S POEMS STAND AS FIRST IN LINE AND MOST important in his oeuvre, two collections of which were published during his lifetime: *Verses* (1896) and *Decorations in Verse and Prose* (1899), the former with a celebrated cover design by the masterful Aubrey Beardsley, likewise a tuberculosis sufferer. Some of Dowson's verse lines are so well known that they have taken on a life of their own – especially outside England – while their author has been consigned to obscurity. Everyone knows the line 'They are not long, the days of wine and roses', but few are aware that it comes from Dowson's poem 'Vitae summa brevis spem nos vetat incohare longam', a title borrowed from Horace. And Margaret Mitchell also found the title for her classic novel *Gone with the Wind* in Dowson's poem entitled 'Non sum qualis eram bonae sub regno Cynarae', likewise taken from Horace. The latter poem, with its repeated alexandrine refrain – 'I have been faithful to thee, Cynara, in my fashion' – is perhaps his best known work.

Taken together, the two collections contain little more than seventy poems, but no authoritative anthology of nineteenth-century English poetry exists that does not include a couple of his verses. The poet's obsession with life's limitations and the inevitability of death, which seamlessly locates his work in the French-English 'black' Romantic tradition, is apparent from several of his titles: 'A Requiem', 'Extreme Unction', 'The Dead Child', 'Villanelle of Acheron', 'In a Breton Cemetery',

'Moritura' and 'A Last Word'. And many other poems swarm
with symbolic allusions to setting suns, floral wreaths, shadow,
decline and decay. But the tone, once again, is more that of the
timeless troubadour singing about the demise of love and life (in
the manner of Du Bellay or Ronsard, or even further back to
Propertius, Horace, or Catullus) than a personal expression of
unhappiness on Dowson's part. Dowson's use of girl's names –
Chloe, Neobule, Lalage or Yvonne, Manon, and of course
Hélène – borrowed from his illustrious and much admired pre-
decessors as fictional names in his poems, reinforces the impression of a universal resignation to fate, though borne with an
evident absence of gravity.

AS IS OFTEN THE CASE WITH ARTISTS (AND NON-ART-
ists for that matter), Ernest Dowson was determined to excel in
a domain for which his talents were less fitting, namely novel
writing. He published two, *A Comedy of Masks* (1893) and *Adrian
Rome* (1899), both written together with Arthur Moore, a friend
from university who was later to become a lawyer. Moore and
Dowson wrote chapters by turns, creating a pair of pallid novels lacking in suspense, both 'plus curieux que beau', which,
in addition to their antiquarian rarity, derive their primary
importance from the occasional references to Dowson's autobiographical background. A born poet, Dowson also spent years
muddling with a solo manuscript for a novel entitled *Madame de
Viole*, but he finally had to admit that it was doomed to remain
a lifeless project and he never finished it. Together with Moore
he worked on two other novels, *Felix Martyr* and *The Passion of
Dr. Ludovicus*; the former was never completed and the latter was

rejected by a series of publishers, a profession Dowson was wont to designate 'the pilfering brotherhood'.

What is interesting about Dowson's failed endeavor to write a successful novel is the years of hope and pleasure he derived from his cordial cooperation with Arthur Moore. The many dozens of letters they exchanged testify to this in an infectious manner. The fact that Dowson was also able to survive for years as a literary translator is perhaps due in like fashion to the fact that he could fall back on an albeit silent 'co-author' who had already given birth to the characters and the story, allowing the translator to dedicate himself entirely to an English translation, using his own stylistic capacities and verbal dexterity. The additional fact that the delivery of a portion of manuscript was rewarded with a guaranteed sum of money, however small, must likewise have been an encouragement. In the last six years of his life, Dowson translated no fewer than seven books, mostly from the French, by authors such as Émile Zola, Honoré de Balzac, Choderlos de Laclos, and the Goncourt brothers, in addition to the memoirs of Cardinal Dubois and the Duc de Richelieu. In collaboration with Dutch-born Alexander Teixeira de Mattos, he was also responsible for the English version of Louis Couperus' novel *Majesteit – Majesty*, published in 1894.

ERNEST DOWSON'S CREATIVE PROSE TALENTS WERE not designed for the symphonic scale of the novel, but were much more at home within the sonata-like scope of the short story. In 1895, Dowson published a small collection entitled *Dilemmas: Stories and Studies in Sentiment*. The majority of these stories have a clearly contemplative bias, while some are better understood as fictionalized essays rather than fully-fledged stories. Characters look back or indeed ahead, but the actions that should move them forward in the present appear for the most part to be absent, apart from the effects of time and fate that dominate their existence. This feature is clearly evident in stories like 'Souvenirs of an Egoist' and 'The Statute of Limitations', both of which already display the notion of retrospective in their titles.

In addition to the five stories included in *Dilemmas* and a few prose poems from his second poetry collection *Decorations*, four stories from the last years of his life were published in magazines. Particular mention must be made in this regard of 'The Dying of Francis Donne' from 1896, which I consider to be an impressive and in equal measure convincing foreshadowing of the end of his own life four years later. But to be able to appreciate this story as a rare preparatory study of Dowson's own deathbed, we should first draw a sketch of his life.

THE OLDER OF TWO SONS, ERNEST CHRISTOPHER Dowson was born on August 2nd, 1867, in what is now known as Lewisham, a south-east London suburb. His father Alfred Dowson was a pathological hypochondriac with a taste for literature and a small family estate in the form of a rented-out dry dock on the banks of the Thames. His mother Annie, née Swan, was a neurotic woman, barely able to cope with everyday life. Both parents passed on their disposition for tuberculosis to their children. Given the fact that the family was always on the move, travelling across the European continent in search of a healthier climate for sickly Alfred, Ernest received no systematic schooling until he was eighteen. Travel provided him with an excellent command of French at a relatively early age, but for an English boy it also led to illogical preferences and developmental gaps. He loved the work of Horace, Propertius, Catullus, Verlaine, Rimbaud, Baudelaire, Henry James, and Swinburne, for example, but managed to reach his thirtieth without ever having read a word of Charles Dickens.

In spite of the inadequacy of his formal education, Dowson's knowledge of French and of the classical languages made enough of an impression on the examiners at Queen's College, Oxford, that he was granted a place. But he used the two years (1886-1888) he spent there to establish a variety of (literary) friendships and little else. Dowson started to publish in literary journals and combated his inherited depressions and increasing concern about his poor health by simply enjoying himself. The boy who had never known a stable home in his youth, was unable to produce the discipline and concentration required for Oxford and after two years of 'keeping up the legal farce' he left behind the prospect of a career in law without too much remorse. He lamented in a letter dated 1889, not long after Oxford: '[I] have almost coughed my lungs out'. He was only twenty-two, but the tuberculosis had him firmly in its grip and was never to let him go.

For the remaining eleven years of his life, Dowson lived at innumerable addresses in England and France. At the start he kept himself busy with office work related to the dry dock 'Dowson & Son', which his father was no longer renting out, but the business didn't flourish and from the middle of the 1890s he left more and more of the work to the local foreman. Around that time his father and mother died in short succession, his father from a suspected overdose of medication; and according to reports, his mother hung herself with a handkerchief from the bars of her bed.

In addition to writing in the evening hours for journals like *Macmillan's Magazine*, *The Century Guild Hobby Horse*, *The Yellow Book*, and *The Savoy* and for the anthologies published by The Rhymers Club, a London poetry association of which he was a member, he mixed and corresponded intensively with literary and artistic contemporaries: W.B. Yeats, Aubrey Beardsley, Charles Conder, John Davidson, John Gray, Richard Le Gallienne, Conal O'Riordan, Arthur Symons, and Oscar Wilde. And not to forget Dowson's colorful and dedicated publisher Leonard Smithers, about whom Oscar Wilde once remarked that he was mad about first editions, especially of women.

As far as women were concerned, Dowson himself was uniquely conflicted. While he was an enthusiastic womanizer, especially among the women in Paris's music hall circuit, he also had a pure, almost religious predilection for twelve-year-old girls. The latter inclination evolved over the years into a personal cult, to which many of his poems bear witness. It reached its climax in a cycle of poems entitled 'Sonnets of a Little Girl', which did not appear in print (with the exception of one poem) until after his death in the posthumous publication *Poetical Works* (1934). The preeminent, real-life object of this ethereal veneration was a girl by the name of Adelaide Foltinowicz, the daughter of a Polish restaurateur on London's Sherwood Street. Dowson saw her there for the first time in November 1889 when she was only eleven years old, and from then on he cherished a chaste and unattainable dream that she would one day share his life. Instead of a wheezing, not very well off, and painfully shy poet, Adelaide opted in 1897 for a German tailor by the name of August Nölte with whom she had three daughters. She died in 1903 at the age of twenty-five as a result of a poorly performed abortion; a markedly prosaic demise for a young woman to whom Ernest Dowson had not only dedicated his finest poems but also his most hopeful expectations.

THE END OF ERNEST DOWSON'S OWN LIFE IN THE LAT-ter part of 1899 and the beginning of 1900 was shameless in its poverty – his parents' estate was firmly trapped in complicated litigation – and in the fact that he was apparently unable to ask one or other of his many friends for help or a provisional place to stay. His drinking habits had become alarming, certainly when one factors in his already vulnerable physical condition, with wine and whiskey making way for foul absinthe. His tattered clothing and neglected teeth rounded out the image of the poet dying in the gutter, as chronicled in many a contemporary publication. After wandering from address to address in Paris and Brittany (including the artist town Pont-Aven), he returned to London in 1899, hoping that he would be better able to conceal his poverty in the big city. The biographer and journalist Robert Harborough Sherard plucked him from the streets around Christmas 1899, critically ill and with a vicious cough. Exhausted, Ernest Dowson breathed his last in the arms of Sherard's wife Marthe on February 23rd, 1900. His final words were addressed to Marthe: 'You are like an angel from heaven.

God bless you.' According to Robert Sherard 'there was no struggle, there was no agony; and the only sign that was given to me was the beautiful calm that settled down, like a brooding dove, upon his tired face. One never saw peace more reposeful on features more ravaged.'

Many have observed parallels over the years between the death of Ernest Dowson and that of John Keats. Not only did they die by coincidence on the same day (February 23rd), more significantly both succumbed to tuberculosis after a (too) short but very productive poetic life, having suffered for years from the unrequited love of a young woman (Adelaide Foltinowicz and Fanny Brawne respectively), who was both close and unattainable in equal measure. 'Like Keats,' Dowson wrote to his old college friend Samuel Smith from Pont-Aven on June 4th, 1897, 'I cannot open her letters for a day or so after they reach me.' Sadly, not one of those letters has survived. Dowson never had a place of his own in which to store such personal papers. Dowson's letters to his '*ferne Geliebte – distant beloved*' Adelaide are likewise lost (in contrast to Keats' magnificent love letters to Fanny Brawne), giving their unfortunate and tragic bond an unreal and intangible character.

ON JANUARY 3RD, 1889, ERNEST DOWSON WROTE TO HIS friend Arthur Moore, the co-author of their novels-in-prog- ress: 'I think if I have a deathbed (wh. I don't desire) I must be reconciled to Rome for the sake of that piece of ritual.' Reconciliation with Rome took place with time to spare on September 25th, 1891, at the Brompton Oratory in London, so there was no apparent reason for Ernest Dowson's deathbed to be so miserable. But what is miserable? In the eyes of those present (the Sherards, a priest, a doctor, plus a bricklayer and his wife who lodged with the Sherards and doubled as servants) it was probably quite impressive. When Mark Longaker, the author of Dowson's first fully-fledged biography, finally traced the former Marthe Sherard (then Mrs Dillon-Jones) to a poor house in August 1939, the first thing the seventy-seven year old woman said to him was: 'I have known great poets: Ernest Dowson died in my arms.' She went on to provide a detailed eyewitness report of the last weeks of the poet's life, forty years after his death. Perhaps in a certain sense all deathbeds are miserable, and that's precisely what makes them so moving and unforgettable.

IN HIS 1896 STORY 'THE DYING OF FRANCIS DONNE', which in terms of form is more of a case study than a story, Ernest Dowson immersed himself in both the run up to a death-bed and the deathbed itself. 1896 was an emotionally charged year for Dowson, following so shortly after the gruesome demise of his recently widowed mother. But death had also left its mark in Dowson's literary surroundings that year with the loss of Paul Verlaine, a man he much admired. Dowson had visited Verlaine on several occasions in Paris and paid tribute to him with a number of sublime translations – included in *Decorations* – and by participating in his funeral procession. In April 1896, inspired perhaps by Verlaine's demise, and with his funereal mood reinforced by his own advancing illness, he described – from his room in Hotel Gloanec in Pont-Aven – the death of the thirty-five year old doctor Francis Donne.

Without dissecting the story exhaustively in search of

parallels with the author's own life, a couple of elements stand out that Dowson could only have described as he did because he himself was getting close to death as a tuberculosis sufferer. The dull, monotonous pain pursuing the body like a shadow, the fleeting exchange of glances with acquaintances who try, out of kindness, not to react too obviously to the sick individual's dramatically changing appearance, other people's hypocritical sympathy, the vitality and complacency of those surrounding the dying person, etc. And then at the very end, the description of Francis Donne crawling out of sight, ashamed, just as Ernest Dowson had tried to make his sickness and his poverty disappear in the big city. Even the alarming dreams and nocturnal hallucinations that Dowson ascribes to Donne must have required a considerable amount of personal experience, as would the effects of mind-expanding (curative) substances.

All things considered, my sense of the quality of Dowson's step-by-step description of Francis Donne's death is inspired by his ability to give lucid and precise expression to the intangible finesses of physical and mental consciousness and their consecutive gradations in a language that sounds as natural and simple as life and death itself. It is this combination of simplicity and charm, of evocativeness and love for detail, and also of honest sentiment and an ambiance of fatality, that makes 'The Dying of Francis Donne' one of the best deathbed stories in world literature. No writer will ever succeed in looking back at his or her own deathbed or at the moment they breathed their last, but I know of few stories or passages from novels in which an author looks ahead to that moment with such understanding and authenticity.

THE BIG PICTURE
AND THE SMALL

Generalists and Specialists in Art History

What kind of art historians do we need more, generalists or specialists? People who have a grasp of the big picture in art, whose broad expertise makes them widely deployable in both geographical and temporal terms? Or people with a genuinely profound understanding of a single well-defined period, artist, or movement in art, who are so expert in the porcelain of the Qianlong period, the oeuvre of Bronzino, or the history of the *Sagrada Familia* in Barcelona that they not only know everything it is humanly possible to know about their subject, but are also capable of extending that accumulated knowledge?

This is more than a theoretical, content-related discussion of what we should consider the most interesting way to look at

art. The answer to this question has potentially serious consequences for the organization of university programs in art history, for the knowledge and skills a student can expect to be
taught in such programs, and for the formulation of the requirements we expect art historians to meet on graduation, bearing
in mind their societal perspectives.

During a symposium organized by the University of
Amsterdam on the occasion of his birthday, Henk van Os,
professor of art history and former director of Amsterdam's
Rijksmuseum turned his attention to this very question. Van
Os's position in the debate can already be discerned from the
title of his presentation – 'The Big Picture in Art History' – and
the polemical slogan that accompanied its publication in the
Dutch weekly *De Groene Amsterdammer* – 'Out of Your Closets!'.
The three propositions upon which his argument is based are
likewise unequivocal:

- Art historians have locked themselves and each
  other up in increasingly narrow specializations.

- Insisting at every opportunity on the autonomy of
  art-historical research has often blinded art historians to the external demand for art-historical
  research and education.

- The radical association of art-historical education
  with research specializations has introduced a completely unnecessary limitation in terms of educational program content.

While there's nothing wrong with generalists as such —
I would be doing myself an injustice if I were to claim the
contrary — I still find it difficult to agree with Van Os's propositions. To start with, I'm crazy about specialists and I'm
convinced they're the heart and brains of every science. Just
as orthodoxy is the core of every religion, specialization is
the primary source of life for every scholarly endeavor. The
problem Van Os rightly points out — the tension between the
academic and the social — is not so much concealed in the
specializations of the specialists as in the fact that they are
locked up in them. There's nothing wrong with specialization
in itself. Specialization is the admissions exam, the academic's swimming certificate as it were. If the twenty-five-year-old
Kenneth Clark — in later years director of London's Victoria
& Albert Museum and a widely respected popularizer of art
history — had not dedicated himself to the study of Leonardo's
drawings and the English Gothic Revival, he would never
have been able to write, lecture, and broadcast on art in all
its manifestations with so much empathy. The now famous
BBC series *Civilisation*, which introduced at least two generations of British TV watchers to the inexhaustible riches of
the history of art, could not have been made on the basis of
accessibility and variedness alone. Conceived and presented
by Kenneth Clark himself, the series excelled in demonstrat-
ing that depth contributed to its quality as much as breadth.
Or to use an example unrelated to art history: if Elias Canetti
had never earned his degree in chemistry with a dissertation
entitled Über die Darstellung des Tertiärbutylcarbinols — *On
the Representation of Tertiary Butyl Carbinols*, he would probably

have been unable to summon the depth of perseverance he needed to complete his all-embracing *Crowds and Power*.

It's all about what specialists ultimately do with their specialist certificates, that they use their skills to practice their craft to completion. It's not only about securing social legitimation for their subject, but first and foremost about putting it into practice in the real world. An architect who graduates in the history of the open kitchen will have to design houses that contain open kitchens side by side with living rooms, basements, bedrooms, and bathrooms. And when they are speaking about their profession, they should also be able to discuss theatres, water towers, office blocks, and bridges, and not only houses with or without open kitchens. So: long live the specialists, but down with the lazy, blinkered variety.

People who know a great deal about one thing, moreover, have an excellent starting position for their further intellectual and professional development – also beyond the realms of academia – and often better than those who know a little about a lot. The literary publisher I worked for until 1998 received many job inquiries, some of them from art historians. In the 1980s, such letters tended to come from people who really knew something about the Italian Renaissance, for example, or French Romanticism, whose French or Italian was also pretty respectable, and who tended to be reasonably well travelled for people in their mid-twenties. In the mid-1990s, however, the letters of application increasingly came from people with degrees in 'Mediterranean Studies' or 'Culture and Media' with a specialization in management. Language skills and a passion for literature were no longer a matter of course. I am personally convinced that this evolution away from specialization towards a sort of general orientation that skims the surface of everything (and thus nothing) has not been a positive one for art historians and their employment outside the university.

In his second proposition, Van Os turns against those art historians who harp on incessantly about the autonomy of their research and teaching, calling upon his colleagues to listen more to the needs of government and the business community. While every call for more cooperation between academy and society enjoys my favor, I'm convinced nevertheless that this is leading us astray. Van Os is not proposing interaction, but rather one-way communication: government and the business world decide what art historians should do with their time. This suggestion, in my opinion, steers art history away from its own moorings, in a precarious attempt to cross over to the employers, patrons, and publishers presumed to be present on the other side of the water.

What happens if art historians succumb to the might of the policy makers and the market? The first step is evident in the present day tendency to describe everything in terms of 'policy'. If a museum lists what it intends to do in the years ahead it's called a 'policy plan'. Publishers refuse manuscripts these days because they don't have a place in their 'publishing policy'. Thinking in 'policy' terms outside the world of governance is a dangerous development because it frustrates the potential clash between professional disciplines. A museum in which only policy-minded people are at work is like a spineless business community in search of consensus, instead of a professional organization in which restorers and curators have different interests, and where the latter have to be on their toes when dealing with exhibition designers, educational staff, and PR people.

I once came across an ad for a job as curator at a municipal museum in the southern part of the Netherlands. Among the job requirements it listed: 'commitment to the discipline' and 'experience with the policy aspects of the domain'. In addition to these magic formulas of officialdom, the job description also stated that candidates would be expected to engage in scholarly research 'in preparation for policy, projects, and publications', yet all that was required in terms of qualification was a vocational (non-university) diploma in art history or the history of civilization. And to add insult to injury, the job being offered was for three days per week only.

Such jobs are in every respect a sort of death knell for art history (and indeed for the museums themselves). If this is the trajectory art historians must follow to secure the social legitimation of their profession, then social legitimation is equivalent to the academic bankruptcy of art history. Art historians should not be forced to choose between academy and society; they should be capable of combining the two as teachers, authors, curators, editors... And in order to establish that connection they need to be on stable ground in both worlds, otherwise the connection will distort irrevocably as one side or the other sinks into the mud.

The same applies *mutatis mutandis* to the influence of the market. Social legitimation and a social function for art historians can be facilitated with some degree of ease by the publication of articles and books. But Van Os's idea that art historians should focus primarily in their writing on what publishers have devised doesn't sound like an attractive answer to the problem. Indeed, the opposite seems much more interesting: art historians – at least the minority among them with writing skills – should devise and write articles and books, collections and biographies, studies and monographs that are so interesting the publishers would be mad not to publish them. If the approach is sound, the style is good, and there is evidence of a writing career with a future, then the subject matter in many instances is not the deciding factor. Publishers are generally happy to engage such authors, and whether they're writing about medieval cathedral construction, the symbol of the tiger in nineteenth-century paintings, contemporary fashion photography, the role of the smile in sculpture through the ages, or the relationship between neo-classicism and totalitarianism in architecture, is often of secondary importance. Style, approach, vision: in short authorial skill, make such subjects and others interesting as a matter of course. And if an author doesn't have these qualities, then listening to 'the market' is a pointless exercise. Indeed, experience teaches us that the market has little if anything to say, especially in countries like the Netherlands, a language area too small to justify the existence of an adequate number of art book publishers.

Van Os's third and final statement argues that the radical association of art-historical teaching and research specializations has resulted in a completely unnecessary limitation in terms of educational program content. The use of words like 'radical' and 'completely unnecessary' make it difficult to disagree with him entirely in this, but in a small country like the Netherlands it should be observed that art history students can take a master's degree at one university – e.g. in a city in which the Italian Renaissance is explored in depth – with a minor at another university at which the history of architecture or fashion theory have a more central place in the program. No one is served by 'completely unnecessary' limitations to program content, but the fact that a student can opt to study a specific topic at a specific university with a national and even international reputation as a 'centre of excellence', seems to me to be a surplus academic value, to say the very least. The most inspiring teachers in graduate and doctoral programs are those who enjoy irrefutable authority in one or more clearly defined domains, preferably on an international scale. It is thus quite acceptable that not every teacher of this sort will be equally at home in every 'corner' of the art-historical world.

The comparison between art-historical generalists and specialists thus gives rise to the following five propositions:

- Long live the specialists, but down with the lazy, blinkered variety.

- Good and active specialists have more to offer than generalists when it comes to the world of government policy and the market.

- Art historians must use the unique power of their profession to resist the present day 'policy mimesis' that has been cast over every discipline like a drab, nondescript veil.

- Art historians shouldn't write what publishers want them to write, but rather what needs to be written (by them), published, and – last but not least - read.

- Excellent teachers in every discipline derive their universal importance from the fact that in a least one academic domain they are lord and master.

In the concluding paragraphs of his argument, Van Os repeats the claim that is also contained in the title of his presentation, namely that art history is primarily about 'major cohesions', about 'the big picture' in art. I can agree with him here on one condition: that he can agree with me in turn that the big picture is a necessary fiction, a narrative to be written by a few brilliant and literarily gifted art historians. But the story of the big picture can't be written, let alone understood, if it is not constructed on the basis of thousands of smaller stories out of which the day-to-day work of art historians is made and into which it ultimately flows. The more exciting, surprising, inspiring. and apposite the little pictures are, the more successful art history's development will be in both academic and societal terms.

Van Os, himself a dedicated specialist in the world of Italian art, whose doctoral dissertation explored the art of painting in fourteenth and fifteenth-century Siena, has evolved into a brilliant art-historical generalist in the second half of his career and acquired a considerable reputation not only in academia, but also in the museum world and on television. His appeal on behalf of 'the big picture' amply and convincingly represents his own academic and social program, but for all the other art historians in the Netherlands and elsewhere, I prefer to stick to my own five propositions.

THE MARCHIONESS TOOK THE NINE O'CLOCK TRAIN

Paul Valéry's Cahiers *as Antinovel*

n September 9th, 1899, in the middle of the night, the French poet, thinker, and essayist Paul Valéry (1871-1945) was unexpectedly confronted by the inner stirrings of a psychological novel. 'Was it the unusually heavy meal that disrupted my sleep,' he later asked himself, 'or the thickness of the cigars – who can tell?' In any event, shortly after retiring to bed at around two o'clock, the author saw an image in his mind's eye of a line with two points: A and B. A became Hortense and B became Henri. And between the two a principle seemed to be at work, a mathematical principle. Henri loved Hortense when he was close to her, and Hortense loved Henri when he was away from her. The relationship and its governing principle provided the first fifteen pages of the novel and the following fifty were dedicated to a description of the lovers' surroundings and friends, and so it continued until the end. The author goes on to assure us that 'An elderly priest and a nude scene' had been included for good measure.

In this satirical description of a novelist's vision, Paul Valéry reveals his contempt for the literary genre of the novel – in addition to his mathematical interests. He wanted nothing to do with the novel and was to spend his entire life keeping his distance from it as both reader and writer. Valéry's primary objection was that novels were forced to deal with elements that were either too particular or too arbitrary. On the aspect of particularity he wrote: 'That is why I always dreamt of a "pure literature", that is to say one founded upon a minimum of direct excitations upon the person and the maximal recourse to the properties intrinsic to language.' And in a now famous passage from his *Cahiers* he takes aim at the arbitrary character of the nineteenth-century novel: 'The countess took the eight o'clock train. The marchioness took the nine o'clock train. I could go on without the least difficulty, introducing variation after variation, just as any imbecile could, including the reader.' Valéry compared fiction, which he understood as the stories he had been forced to fabricate under the tyranny of children, to a kaleidoscope: 'A few pieces of colored glass, three little mirrors, and turn at will. Words, images, symmetries.'

Harsh words indeed, aimed at a literary genre that was highly favored in his day (and even more in ours), by both the public and the literary critics, and as a result the most dominant form of artistic expression among writers. Valéry was also well aware that he was not suited to writing novels. 'I try to neglect what the novel tries to magnify, and vice versa,' he once wrote, in his typically cryptic style. He declared that he did not have the slowness necessary for writing novels and could not reconcile himself to the assumptions required in telling even the simplest of stories: 'To write novels you need to understand people as well-defined entities or elements. "He did this. She said that." One easily forgets that it is precisely "did" and "said" and "that" that describe and construct He and She in every possible instance.' Such statements, which define Paul Valéry's relationship with the novel and thereby with a not insignificant portion of the literature of his time, suggest that he was too much of a philosopher to write novels, that he focused too much on language and the human mind to occupy himself with the illusions and diversions of the invented world of the novel. At the same time, however, his philosophical, logical and mathematical attitude did not prevent him from being a great poet, and poems like 'La Jeune Parque' and 'Le Cimetière marin' testify that his need for precision did not stand in the way of creating endless ambiguities.

The only work of Valéry that has been described for the sake of convenience in terms of a novel is his short text *La Soirée avec Monsieur Teste – An Evening with Mr Teste*, constructed along narrative lines and originally published in 1896. Instead of being a (partial) novel, however, the text in question introduces a so-called 'friend' – the 'I' figure – of a character created by Valéry as a sounding board for his philosophical reflections on the perfect intellect, the operation of the independent human mind that functions in complete autonomy from the outside world. In everything, even Mr. Teste's shallowest sigh, the focus for him and his friend – who serves as chronicler – is on the rules and the forms of his mind. At the end of the account, just before Mr. Teste falls asleep in his bed with the nameless narrator listening at his side in the light of a flickering candle, the main character says: 'I exist and see myself; I see how I see myself, etc... Let us sharpen our thoughts.'

It would perhaps be simplistic and mundanely biographical to identify Teste with his maker, but the narrator's final words nevertheless bring us close to the central principle at work in Paul Valéry's oeuvre. 'To think sharp' (and not to invent stories about non-existent people) was foundational to the French author's life's work. And the preeminent place to locate the latter is in the *Cahiers*, the notebooks Valéry kept from 1894 until his death in 1945, on which he worked almost every day. Valéry offers a fine definition of the said foundation: I stop thinking as I think to consider what I'm thinking, and then I think about it.

At first sight, the *Cahiers* are extremely far removed from the entire idea of a novel, at least in the form that Valéry ridiculed with his dream anecdote. They can only be described as a 'dream book', insofar as they are the embodiment of the pursuit of the one, ideal, ultimate book that charts every possibility of the human mind, thereby overshadowing every other book. Such an endeavor must, by definition, remain a dream, although the 26,600 pages of the *Cahiers*, spread over more than 260 notebooks, has to be regarded as the most far-reaching venture in this direction by any single person. But the expression 'dream book' is incorrect on two different levels. In the first place, because the notes in question were written during that part of the day when the author tended to be most awake, i.e. between four and eight-thirty in the morning. In the second place because they were never intended to be a book, let alone a finished book, and they have never been published as such, either in French or in translation. The only more or less complete version thus far of these daybreak ruminations, representing more than half a century of writing, is a facsimile edition of the manuscript of all the *Cahiers*, which appeared between 1957 and 1961 in twenty-nine folio volumes. The print run was limited to one thousand copies.

But if Valéry's *Cahiers* are so far removed from the novel and are, in a sense, its antithesis, how should the literary reader approach them after a century and a half of conditioning, primarily by the novel? And if they don't contain characters or events, what are they about?

IN AN ESSAY SUCH AS THIS, THE NEXT LOGICAL STEP would be to say a little more about the author's background, something along the following lines: Paul Valéry was born on October 30th, 1871; or: Paul Valéry first saw the light of day on May 12th, 1869; or what about: Paul Valéry came into the world on February 11th, 1872? But the words of the author's own reproof quoted above rise up to confront us: 'I could go on without the least difficulty, introducing variation after variation, just as any imbecile could, including the reader.' In other words: an introduction to Paul Valéry's *Cahiers*, and even a degree of insight into their content, does not oblige us to review the author's biographical details. Indeed, we would do the *Cahiers* a serious injustice if we were to approach them from a biographical perspective. The *Cahiers* are part of a timeless tradition in which Leonardo da Vinci's approximately 15,000 pages of notes must also be located, and the fact that three centuries stand between these two thinkers is of no importance when it comes to the value of either's written work. It goes without saying that Paul Valéry – like everyone else – had a birthplace, a childhood, school and university experience, later a family life (and several mistresses), and that he corresponded with writers and publishers, all easily summarized in a more or less detailed list of essential public and private events. But the *Cahiers* are of a different order. They locate us far offshore, in the remotest regions of the intellect. Throughout his adult life, for a total of fifty-one years, Paul Valéry sat down in his study in the early hours of the morning, in the crow's-nest, as it were, of his conscious mind, to commit his thoughts to paper.

But the question remains: what are all those thoughts about, all 26,600 pages worth? The answer: nothing, they simply 'are'. His thoughts are exercises, trial runs. And these 'thought exercises' relate to a variety of domains: mathematics, philosophy, physics, psychology, linguistics, astronomy, history, literature, in short every possible domain. The *Cahiers* cannot thus be considered a diary in which events are described. 'Events,' Valéry noted, 'are the spray of things, but I'm interested in the sea.' It is for this reason that the author observed *himself* from his metaphorical crow's-nest rather than what was going on around him, as he compelled his mind from the conscious to the unconscious and back again, etc. The forms in which Valéry chose to cast his daily observations are legion: analyses, outlines, fantasies, comparisons, aphorisms, tables, syllogisms, formulas, watercolors, definitions. Every possible instrument a mind has at its disposal is used to report its workings on paper.

It goes without saying that an enterprise such as the *Cahiers*, constantly shifting from one domain to another and from one form to another, is difficult to grasp and contain, even for its author. Only four years after he started his note taking, Valéry endeavored to organize the material in terms of theme and chronology, already an almost impossible task that he was to attempt on a number of occasions in later years with the assistance of a secretary or two, but to no avail. The various providers of selections from the *Cahiers*, in particular Judith Robinson-Valéry's two volume Pléiade edition, have likewise been unsuccessful. That edition presents us with a thematic arrangement of roughly one tenth of the total material. This has two major disadvantages: it does not offer a chronological – let alone logical – picture of the development of Valéry's ideas on a given subject, and the picture it does provide is on average only 10% complete. The reader is also expected to do without Valéry's drawings, watercolors, and illustrations that accompany the original notes.

A start was made in 1987 on a new – in fact the first – printed edition of the *Cahiers*, which attempted in typographical terms to do as much justice as possible to the original manuscripts. A praiseworthy ambition in itself, but this publication is also lacking on another level, not only on account of the disconcertingly bad reproductions of the drawings and watercolors with which Valéry illustrated his notes, but something more fundamental. Valéry wrote in 1905: 'Everything written in these notebooks of mine refuses to be definitive by its very nature.' And in 1921 he wrote: 'I describe here the ideas that occur to me. But that does not mean that I accept them. This is their initial state.' In other words: there is something fundamentally wrong going on when we attempt to cast these living, hand-written ideas in a fixed, stable, and definitive printed form.

If there is one constant theme to be observed in the *Cahiers* it's the fact that the author was obsessed with testing, maintaining, and cultivating the potential of the human mind. He often returned to earlier notes and added further elaborations, where necessary on separate sheets of paper which he then inserted in the notebooks. The relentlessly mobile, inexhaustible and dynamic character of the *Cahiers* inclined Valéry expert S. Dresden to insist that we should not see them as *a work* but as *work-in-progress*, and we thus do an injustice to the *Cahiers* when we settle for a printed edition – with an abundance of footnotes and commentary – and thereby suggest that we have achieved an end result. In so doing we transform the *Cahiers* into a sort of intellectual idol, which – like every idol – inspires passive admiration rather than active participation in the possibilities this stream of living ideas holds out to us.

IT SHOULD BE CLEAR BY NOW THAT PAUL VALÉRY'S *Cahiers* are more or less the opposite of a novel. They contain no characters, no storyline, no scenes; they do not establish a fictional world and there is no narrator. Taken together and in their various subdivisions, the notes are essentially fragmentary, perhaps even unfinishable, and lack any form of temporal perspective. In short: the *Cahiers* are the antinovel par excellence, an antinovel that – as we have seen – repeatedly polemicizes the novel genre and even ridicules it.

Nevertheless, an almost diabolical temptation inclines me to apply the principle of meeting extremes and test the idea that the *Cahiers* are so far removed from the traditional novel that they ultimately come close to it at its opposite end, as it were, in its more modernistic incarnation. Just as James Joyce's *Ulysses* employs a stream of consciousness to describe a single day in the life of Stephen Dedalus, and just as Marcel Proust's *À la recherche du temps perdu* constructs an immense remembered world replete with characters and events on the basis of a single memory of a taste and a smell, perhaps – and with a considerable mental leap – we can classify the *Cahiers* as the most modernistic novel ever written, a novel that uses a 'stream of intelligence' to describe the life of a single human mind, from age twenty-two to its passing at seventy-three. That human mind, which is simultaneously the narrator of the 26,600 page novel, does not dig around in its autobiographical memory – as Proust's main character does – but tries to explore the finesses of its own consciousness and extend its boundaries. And in contrast to Joyce, the main character in Valéry's *Cahiers* is more in tune with Penelope than with Odysseus. Every morning between four and eight-thirty – the hour between lamp and sun as Valéry liked to call it – this mind weaves itself a new robe, not because it needs one, but because it needs to exercise itself by making something of itself and for itself each day while excluding the rest of the world.

And what about the reader of this antinovel, the reader accustomed to characters and scenes, who wants to know what happens next, whether Henri still loves Hortense more when she's close to him, and Hortense still loves Henri more when he's far from her? Rest assured, the reader won't have time to be bored. Every immersion in Paul Valéry's *Cahiers* is a new and exhilarating adventure, complete with philosophical duels, intellectual flirtations, historical battles, mathematical reconciliations and literary discoveries. But I have to admit, there's no elderly priest or nude scene.

PHOTOGRAPHY AND AUTOBIOGRAPHY

Kousbroek's Photosynthesis as
Blending with the Reader

A thirty-nine-year-old woman leafing through a lingerie catalog also sees what a boy of twelve sees when doing the same thing: the same shoulder straps, the same cups, the same curves. But if you ask the woman and the boy which section they prefer and why, then it quickly becomes evident that they've been looking at the catalog very differently. Something similar can be said about the photos selected by Rudy Kousbroek for a variety of Dutch newspapers, as point of departure for a short personal essay. The column in question bore the title *'Fotosynthese – Photosynthesis'*, a term that gradually evolved into a sort of genre designation for a highly personal combination of looking at and reflecting on a photograph. Kousbroek's brief essays, limited by size restrictions to a maximum of one thousand words or thereabouts, were published in collected form for the first time in 2003 under the title *Opgespoorde wonderen – Recovered Miracles*. A second collection appeared under the title *Verborgen verwantschappen – Hidden Kinships* in 2005. And after the publication of a third volume in 2007, with the equally programmatic title *Het raadsel der herkenning – The Riddle of Recognition*, a posthumous collection of all 196 'photosynthesis' columns was published in 2010 under the original title *Opgespoorde wonderen – Recovered Miracles*, this time with the subtitle: *De fotosyntheses verzameld – Photosynthesis Collected*. An exploration of this collection reveals that the photos selected by Kousbroek for his columns can be roughly divided into two categories.

The most eye-catching category is that of the 'remarkable' photo. Take, for example, the shot of three émouleurs – knife-grinders – in a row, flat on their bellies on a rotating whetstone. The photo was taken in a grindery in the French town of Thiers (Puy de Dôme), and would appear to stem from the beginning of the twentieth century. While the image is unusual in itself, it is made all the more remarkable by the fact that each of the grinders has a dog lying on his legs. Kousbroek's research in the local knife museum (Musée de la Coutellerie) revealed that the émouleurs – whose work was hard and exhausting – had trained their dogs to lie on their legs to keep them warm in the winter.

Kousbroek attaches an essay to this curious tableau, borrowed in part from the work of Jorge Luis Borges. But while his text is worthy in itself, the uniqueness of this particular 'photosynthesis' is in fact to be located in the discovery of the stunning photograph. Similar extraordinary discoveries are scattered here and there throughout the collection, among them a photo of a more than thirty-foot-tall bell hanging in a stone and wood frame in the middle of the Burmese jungle and overgrown with vegetation, or a photo by Eli Lotar of thirty or so cloven-hoofed animal legs, severed and standing against the wall of a Paris abattoir, elegant and horrifying at the same time. In both instances, the photo – like that of the émouleurs – is good for at least half of what makes the author's photosynthesis attractive.

But then we come to the second category of photos, and as far as I'm concerned it's here that Kousbroek's photo-essays display their true vigor and charisma. The photos in question are the sort most of us come across from time to time, photos in which nothing much is apparently going on: a cat, a couple of donkeys, rows of chairs, a British postage stamp, a matador with a bull, a jellyfish, a man on a footbridge, and so forth. Such photos appear at 'first sight' to be pretty mundane, nothing special, but then Kousbroek sets about exposing their 'second sight' in his accom-

Photo Sarah Hart, 1976

panying essay. For the author, that 'second sight' is the secret of the photo, the riddle he needs to solve in a thousand words or less. It's the intense, associative way of looking that Kousbroek lets loose on these 'ordinary' photos that makes me think of the twelve-year-old boy looking at a lingerie catalog. Looking isn't limited to observing, it's also suggestion, imagination, a glance into a mysterious world.

What Kousbroek manages to do with a photo of a house under a huge apple tree or one of the Paris café La Place Blanche has something in common with pornography. He doesn't only look, he feasts his eyes with enormous intensity on everyday or historical reality in all its nakedness. He does not only describe what he sees, he visualizes all the beautiful, sad, and exciting things the photo makes him think about, things the photo only hints at, if at all. It might sound weird, but it's as if the writer is masturbating his mind. But while the latter metaphor may have its merits, it does not lead us to the core of Kousbroek's method, around which two additional questions plainly circle.

Let's begin with the title of the third compilation of photo essays, *The Riddle of Recognition*. What is the riddle the author recognizes in some images that is apparently absent in others? Kousbroek himself also devotes more time to this question here in the third volume than in the first two. His answer in a nutshell is that a photo has to contain an unintentional strangeness, which captures, either playfully or profoundly, one of life's great secrets (love, death…). Nonchalant and fabricated images are excluded; the secret has to be mysterious and impenetrable, but it also has to be unexpected.

Kousbroek was inspired to formulate this credo when he was looking at a photo of the bloodstained tunic of Habsburg Crown Prince Franz Ferdinand, the tunic he was wearing during his fateful visit to Sarajevo on June 28th, 1914 when he and his consort Sophie von Hohenberg were shot and killed by

Unknown photographer, 1914

the Serbian nationalist Gavrilo Princip. A number of photos of the event exist – taken immediately before or immediately after the shooting – and there are detailed eye-witness testimonies, but for Kousbroek this bloodstained garment reveals the secret of death, hidden in an article of clothing, more than any other memento of the occasion: 'Not staged or intentional, but found – as if it wormed its way in.'

The second question that has an important role to play in Kousbroek's photosynthesis can also be posed on the basis of the same bloodstained tunic. The first sentence of the accompanying essay runs: 'I have known this photo since I was twelve.' It was included in a pre-war photo album entitled *Zwanzig Jahre Weltgeschichte – Twenty Years of World History*, and it was here that the young Kousbroek first encountered the secret of death as he explored recent world history: 'When I first saw the photo in question, I remember how I tried to imagine that a real person had once inhabited this garment.'

Most of the photos Kousbroek subjects to his photosynthesis have such an autobiographical dimension, something extra, a third temporal layer. We begin with the time in which the photo was taken, with the world that time evokes. Then we have the present time, the now in which the author engages the photo and forms associations and reflections. But in between there is an intermediate layer, the time at which Kousbroek first saw the photo in question, or experienced the phenomenon it portrays most intensely. This autobiographical dimension serves to detach the images he is discussing from the page as it were, and transform them for the observer into plausible images with which they too can empathize. Taken together, these three dimensions also make it possible to read *Recovered Miracles* as an autobiography of Rudy Kousbroek, in spite of the fact that it is actually a collection of short essays illustrated with photographs.

SOME PEOPLE HAVE A PHOTOGRAPHIC MEMORY. IN Rudy Kousbroek's case it's not so much the precision of his memories that impresses most, but the way he combines photography and memory in a unique relationship. Photographs for Kousbroek are primarily instruments that serve to carry us through time, not only to the moment at which the given photo was taken, but also, and more importantly, to moments in his own life with which the photo is directly or indirectly related. The photos in *The Riddle of Recognition*, for example, are more than just reproductions of something that once actually existed or happened; in the hands of Kousbroek they become embodiments of his own memories.

Kousbroek already employed the technique of pinning his reflections to photos and other images in earlier collections of essays (e.g. *Het meer der herinnering – The Lake of Remembrance* and *De vrolijke wanhoop – Cheerful Despair*). He even published an entire novel based on associations with nineteenth-century etchings (*Vincent en het geheim van zijn vaders lichaam – Vincent and the Secret of His Father's Body*). In short, the interplay between image, memory, and imagination has been a constant feature of his work for many years. But perhaps assisted by the restricted number of words and favored by the generous format of the photos, Kousbroek's three photosynthesis compilations have, in my opinion, realized one of their author's long cherished ideals: a highly personal time machine in book form; a time machine in word and image that could transport him on command to the origins of certain marvels that have preoccupied him all his life; a time machine that also allowed him to travel back to precious and memorable people and events in his own life. And the finest aspect of Rudy Kousbroek's photo-essay time machine is that there's room for a pillion rider next to the driver, namely the reader.

IN MOST CASES THERE'S A CLEAR DIFFERENCE BETWEEN the writer of a book and its reader. The former has an idea and casts it in words, the latter consumes it and in the best case scenario it becomes part of him or her. But the intensity of Kousbroek's historical, autobiographical, and essayistic empathy with the photos he chooses to comment on create a situation in which the writer and the reader gradually merge. His father becomes my father, his idyllic memories become my imagined experiences, his fantasies about an island inhabited only by girls seize retroactive control of my

Photo Max Emden, circa 1937

boyhood dreams. The photosynthesis that works its magic in the hands of Rudy Kousbroek isn't only a time machine, it's a machine that runs back and forth between the memory and the imagination of the author on the one hand, and the corresponding places in the heart and mind of the reader.

With Rudy Kousbroek in the driver's seat and the reader in his sidecar, the past not only becomes more attractive than the present – more precious and more interesting – it also becomes more real compared to the surrounding reality of the here and now. And when it comes to time travelers – some at least, with the famed but nameless hero from H.G. Wells' *The Time Machine* as the finest example – the more they discover of the past, the more they are inclined to dwell there, where they are in complete control. The perfect amalgamation of photography and autobiography in the photosynthesis compilations of Rudy Kousbroek is already something unique, but the fact that the reader can fully participate in that amalgamation is an outright miracle.

TO WED OR NOT TO WED

The Marital World of Delmore Schwartz

an marriage be compared with anything? The British writer J.M. Barrie once made an amusing attempt in *My Lady Nicotine*, with a chapter entitled 'Smoking and Matrimony Compared'. But the truth, I suspect, is that marriage is an entirely unique phenomenon, and that not only its thrills, but more importantly its throes, are hard to parallel with anything else. The latter category, marriage and its miseries, is aptly exemplified in the life of American poet and author Delmore Schwartz (1913-1966).

To begin with, the stars governing his decades of experimenting with the phenomenon appear to have been particularly ill-aligned. On one occasion in 1919 – when he was five years old – Delmore's parents woke him in the middle of the night to ask which of the two he would choose now that they had decided to separate. An eight year via dolorosa was to follow, until his mother finally agreed to the divorce his father had been begging for.

With a view to Delmore's own marital prospects, his maternal grandmother Hannah Nathanson showered him with compelling advice from the moment he hit puberty. A nice Jewish girl, that was the message, and preferably one with plenty of money. 'The best is none too good for you,' she used to add. As far as Delmore's mother was concerned, such a creature probably didn't exist, while his father cherished different ambitions for his son, primarily of the social and financial variety. An obsession with being faithful to one's Jewish roots by arranging the ideal marriage and a fixation on moving up in the world were not exactly unique to the Schwartzes. In the 1920s and 1930s, they were the primary preoccupations of the first generation of Jewish immigrants to the United States, and well-intended as they may have been, these preoccupations often became the misery of their children's lives. When Arthur Miller's mother told her father in 1940 that his grandson had decided to marry a non-Jewish girl, for example, the old man grabbed a heavy alarm clock that happened to be on a table nearby and hurled it across the room at his daughter's head. Fortunately he missed, but only by a hair's breadth.

The Schwartzes were no better. Perhaps they sensed that their son Delmore's lengthy relationship with Gertrude Buckman, which started in 1933 when he was nineteen, ultimately lacked true passion. Around the time they first met Delmore called her 'a kind of Dutch beauty', but two years later he noted coolly in his diary: 'I know at least two girls I would rather marry'. In the spring of 1938, however, he managed to convince himself, his intended, and her parents to support the idea of a wedding.

His own mother, Rose Schwartz née Nathanson, was less easy to convince, euphemistically spoken. She started by threatening suicide if he went ahead with the wedding plans, and then accused him in no uncertain terms of cruelty for abandoning her. On the day of the wedding itself – June 14th, 1938 – Rose claimed to be sick and made an enormous fuss about being carried up the stairs of the synagogue. As a result, the rabbi who was to officiate at the wedding became pressed for time – he was scheduled to preside at a funeral immediately afterwards – and the entire Buckman family was left sniveling and miserable. They were far from impressed with their darling Gertrude's choice of husband: a Harvard dropout with no fixed income who had set his sights on a career in writing.

Delmore's mother must have been the ultimate 'Jewish mother from hell', a deadly combination of the endearing and the unbearable; someone you can no longer deal with after a certain moment, but also someone you can't just leave in the lurch. In Rose's case, the unbearable finally won the battle. When she died in the fall of 1962, Delmore hadn't seen her in a year. He refused to attend the funeral, but sent flowers with a card quoting from a poem by James Joyce: 'O mother forsaken, forgive your son', adapted in terms of gender to fit the occasion. I'm not aware if Delmore's three-year-younger brother Kenneth attended the funeral. But it is known that when Kenneth's turn came – a few years after Delmore's – to inform

Rose Schwartz of his forthcoming marriage, his mother spoke the following unforgettable words: 'He would have been better off in Buchenwald than married to that woman.'

THE SCHWARTZ FAMILY'S MERCILESS APPROACH TO the subject of marriage had everything to do with the disastrous marriage of Mr. and Mrs. Schwartz. Harry Schwartz and Rose Nathanson, both Romanian Jews whose families had emigrated to America only a few years earlier, met each other in 1909, married a couple of years later, and moved into a succession of apartments of varying dimensions in Brooklyn. Harry, according to reports, was intent on not having children and early in their marriage his wife was also apparently unable to conceive. Without her husband's knowledge, however, Rose had an operation when Harry was on a business trip and fell pregnant unexpectedly shortly after his return. Their son Delmore David was born on December 8th, 1913, but the problems started not long after the birth of Kenneth three years later: tensions, arguments, separation. The threat of lawyers quickly became a reality and the battle commenced. Trial separation was followed by a very brief reunification – all to no avail.

When Delmore was seven, he joined his mother, an aunt, and a few of their friends on a mid summer day trip to Long Island. On the way back, his mother suddenly noticed her husband's car parked in front of a roadside restaurant. She insisted that everyone wait for her and marched into the restaurant hand in hand with Delmore. Harry was having dinner with another woman. A terrible scene followed as the waiters and

diners witnessed a flood of accusations from Rose and the rau-
cous dismissal of her husband's new girlfriend as a whore.

Delmore's relationship with his father was just as strange
as with his mother. At one point in the heat of the marital battle,
Harry offered Rose the sum of $75,000 for permanent custody
over his eldest son, which, while it may have testified to a some-
what unusual way of looking at the world, also said something
about the extent of his paternal love. But with Delmore's literary interests and ambitions his father did not sympathize much,
although he was definitely proud when his eldest's first poems
started to appear in print.

The stock market crash of 1929 put an end to Harry's
chances of building a new life with his new partner and in less
than a year his heart succumbed to the stress. Harry Schwartz'
estate took on ever more mythical proportions after his death,
but it quickly evaporated in a mist of mismanagement, legal speculation, notarial obscurity, and other such confusion. Delmore
was thus to live his entire life in poverty, barely eking out an
existence on scholarships, appointments at various universities,
fees for book reviews, articles and poems, and advances from his
lifelong publisher James Laughlin of New Directions for books
that were written with difficulty and always with endless delay.

He had learned from his parents, who were relatively well-
to-do in the few years they were together, that money didn't
guarantee a happy marriage. But as Delmore was to learn from
his own two marriages, a lack of money also has its shortcomings. His first marriage to Gertrude Buckman, who had similar
literary ambitions, was a struggle in every respect and ended in
divorce in 1944. Divorce wasn't simple in those days, because

the state of New York only allowed it on the basis of adultery. So they invited a couple of friends to a hotel where they were supposed to burst into Delmore's room at a pre-arranged moment and catch him in the act, as it were. The plan was good, but they had trouble finding a woman willing to play the adulterous girlfriend. Gertrude ended up playing the role herself, allowing their friends to declare with conviction (backed up by Delmore) that they had indeed seen a woman run into the bathroom.

In the same year, 1944, Delmore Schwartz met the woman who was to be his second wife, the writer and editor Elizabeth Pollett. 'Love exists only when it is unrequited,' Delmore noted at the time in the margin of a book of Rilke poems. If his words were genuine, then he was clearly taking an extra risk by attempting marriage for a second time, certainly after all the misery he had experienced in that department in his immediate entourage. They lived together for a while and finally tied the knot on June 10th, 1949. But the trial run didn't help. Their marriage came to an end in 1955 after six years of depression, fits of temper and – especially in the latter period – pure paranoia. As Delmore himself observed: 'I got married the second time, in the way that, when a murder is committed, crackpots turn up at the police station to confess the crime.'

SKETCHING A PORTRAIT OF DELMORE SCHWARTZ ON the basis of a single theme – marriage – may not be entirely fair, although it was clearly a dominant motif in his life. I could have based a biographical article about him on alterative themes such as alcohol, depression, Jewish identity, insomnia, or lack of money, and with as much justification. All things considered, it's hard to find a positive line of approach to the figure of Delmore Schwartz. Even the recognition he was given as a writer at different times in his life, for his poems, critical reviews, essays, and short stories – he wrote several novels, but none of them passed the (chaotic) manuscript stage –, has something sad about it. At the end of his life he was close to becoming a living literary legend, unapproachable, admired from a distance by the younger post-war generation (and immortalized by Saul Bellow as the tragic main character in *Humboldt's Gift*). But the terrible truth remains that Schwartz' poetry (including collections such as *Genesis* from 1943 and *Summer Knowledge* from 1959) never lived up to the promise of the precocious work of his youth, such as his insomnia poem 'In the Naked Bed, in Plato's Cave' or the equally autobiographical 'The Heavy Bear'. His later stories (in *The World is a Wedding* from 1948 and in *Successful Love and Other Stories* from 1961) likewise pale in comparison with his very first short story, written at the age of twenty-one, 3,500 words with the sublime title 'In Dreams Begin Responsibilities'. And what was its subject? You've guessed it: the attitude of a twenty-one-year-old narrator to the marriage of his parents.

VLADIMIR NABOKOV CONSIDERED 'IN DREAMS BEGIN Responsibilities' one of his 'half a dozen favorites in modern literature'. Such a remark, of course, can only be properly appreciated if you know the titles and authors of the other five, but it nonetheless remains disinterested praise from a master of prose literature. Delmore Schwartz wrote the story in a single July weekend in 1935 when he was living in rooms near New York's Washington Square. The story covers a day in the life of his parents, namely Sunday June 12ᵗʰ, 1909, the day his father asked his mother to marry him.

The story was first published in the first edition of the journal *Partisan Review* (volume 4, issue 1), which had recently been reestablished after exchanging its links with the Communist Party for a less charged, but still clearly left-oriented, social-critical engagement. In addition to 'In Dreams...' the issue also contained poetry by Wallace Stevens and James Agee, an essay by Edmund Wilson on the political dimension in the novels of Gustave Flaubert, a political prose poem by Pablo Picasso, an essay on Ignazio Silone, a critical article by Dwight MacDonald on the first thirteen years of *The New Yorker*, a theatre chronicle by Mary McCarthy, seven book reviews, and a readers discussion forum. The prominent presence of the young Delmore Schwartz in such illustrious company clearly underlines the fact that he, as a writer, was part of the intelligentsia – more so indeed than a Hemingway or a Dos Passos – such that the later *New York Times* critic Anatole Broyard would be fully justified in describing him as 'the typical New York intellectual of the forties'.

But this was still a long way off in 1935, and it was to take years before the story was published in book form by the progressive publisher New Directions together with poems and a theatre piece in verse. For the time being, we're still dealing with the stripling Harvard dropout who decided on a whim just before his final exams to call it a day as far as university was concerned, head for New York, and start a career in writing.

Schwartz owned a copy of the 1933 Macmillan edition of William Butler Yeats' *Collected Poems* and it was here that he found the title for his story. Yeats uses the words 'In dreams begin responsibilities' as an epigraph in his 1914 collection *Responsibilities* ascribing them to an 'old play'. Schwartz managed to send Yeats a copy of his New Directions collection – likewise entitled *In Dreams Begin Responsibilities* – in December 1938. Unfortunately the elderly poet died a few weeks later on January 28th, 1939, making it unlikely that he would have seen or read it. In any event, there is no record of a reaction from Yeats.

'I THINK IT IS THE YEAR 1909. I FEEL AS IF I WERE IN A motion picture theatre, the long arm of light crossing the darkness and spinning, my eyes fixed on the screen.' The narrator in 'In Dreams...' is watching a silent movie, the black and white variety scored by age. 'It is Sunday afternoon, June 12th, 1909, and my father is walking down the quiet streets of Brooklyn on his way to visit my mother.' His collar is a little too tight for such a sunny Sunday afternoon and he's also a little too self-assured, thinking about all the exciting things awaiting him at his fiancées house. In the meantime, the narrator sinks deeper into his cinema chair as the theater's organist renders the audience's emotions to perfection. The narrator senses a salutary anonymity, and the film takes possession of him like a narcotic.

From the opening paragraphs onwards, 'In Dreams...' unfurls as a fated love story, which the narrator simply observes, unable to intervene. His father arrives too early at the home of his intended, still not sure if he will ask her to marry him. The girl's father also has his doubts. Conversations are stilted and minor misunderstandings determine the awkwardness of the atmosphere. His father and mother decide to head out for the day to fashionable Coney Island. On the way they talk at cross-purposes or try to impress one another. The narrator is overcome by the sadness of what he sees and bursts into tears, much to the annoyance of the other filmgoers.

On Coney Island, the American flag flutters in the summer breeze while the 'fatal, merciless, passionate ocean' crashes onto the shore in the blazing sunlight. His parents clearly have so little feeling for their environment and for each other that the narrator is moved to tears once again. 'There, there, all of this is only a movie, young man, only a movie,' an elderly woman tries to reassure him, but his tears are so intense he's forced to withdraw to the cinema restrooms to calm down.

When he returns to his place he has the feeling he's looking down from the fiftieth floor of a skyscraper watching his father and mother on a merry-go-round, barely able to enjoy the experience. Then, in search of a bite to eat, they find themselves a needlessly expensive restaurant. A palm-court orchestra entertains the diners, and moved by the stirring rhythm of a waltz, his father suddenly and impulsively pops the question after bragging at length about his future prospects. His mother is confused and bursts into tears. At this point the narrator can no longer control himself. He jumps to his feet and starts shouting at the screen: 'Don't do it! It's not too late to change your minds, both of you. Nothing good will come of it, only remorse, hatred, scandal, and two children whose characters are monstrous.' The audience has had enough of the young man's interruptions and an attendant appears who informs the narrator that he'll be asked to leave if he doesn't return to his seat immediately.

Two short concluding scenes round off the story. The first

takes place in a photographer's studio where the narrator's parents are intent on having a photo taken to immortalize the day on which his father proposed to his mother. The result of endless trial shots, moving around, adjusted seating, quibbling, and considerable impatience is a photograph in which his father has a grimace on his face and his mother is attempting to look cheerful but to no avail. The second takes place in the tent of an 'oriental' fortune-teller, which his mother insists on entering in spite of his father's protest. The narrator now begins to get so loudly involved with what's happening on the screen that the attendant appears once again and throws him out of the cinema into the cold light of day. At this point he wakes up in his own bed. It's the morning of his twenty-first birthday.

IT WOULD MAKE LITTLE SENSE IN OUR PRESENT CONtext to try to explore all the symbols and allusions this story contains. There's also no need to do so since the story itself is perfectly clear and simple. The various temporal layers are woven together with flawless virtuosity and the combination of the cinema setting with the feverish effects of a narcotic – or with a classical dream sequence – is totally unaffected. The sketch of a first generation immigrant couple, penned by their own son, is nothing short of merciless, focusing on their bourgeois ambitions, their material obsessions, their patriotic affinity with all things American, in parallel with their prospectless and ill-considered decision to marry. 'In Dreams Begin Responsibilities' is Delmore Schwartz' first story and at the same time his best. And as observed above, it is certainly one of the most beautiful stories ever written about marriage.

Delmore Schwartz gave the manuscript of 'In Dreams...' to his mother to read when she was on a visit. We know how she reacted because she scribbled her thoughts on the back of the original, which can be found among the author's as yet unclassified papers in the Beinecke Collection of Yale University:

Dear Delmore,

If there is another word besides wonderful I dont know. I dont remember telling you all these so accurate. Please save this story and bring it home for me. There are moments in my life, that I believe all my struggles are worth wile.

Mother

Judging by this heartrending compliment, Delmore's description of that one day in the life of his parents had clearly struck a chord. Perhaps the story's virtues also lie in the fact that it is so powerfully true to life in spite of its artificial and dreamlike structure, so much so that even his mother was prompted to praise its accuracy.

But there's one peculiar detail in 'In Dreams Begin Responsibilities' that appears to have gone unnoticed. Neither his biographer James Atlas, nor Schwartz expert Richard MacDougall, nor Irving Howe – who wrote an introduction to a later edition of the collection – nor any other text or analysis I've read in relation to this story appear to be aware that the Sunday on which Delmore Schwartz' father proposed to his mother (Sunday June 12th,1909) never existed. June 12th, 1909, was in fact a Saturday. Did the author just pick a date at random in June 1909 and call it a Sunday? Did he 'christen' his parent's daytrip on the Jewish Sabbath, relocating it to a Sunday afternoon for the sake of his readers? Or did he introduce this subtle fictionalizing calendar shift to demonstrate that no matter how much you try to project yourself into the marriage of your parents, its reality will always escape you? Was he trying to say that there's no reality to describe after the event, only memory, and that memory belongs by definition to the domain of fiction? If only for that reason, a marriage cannot easily be compared to something else, and especially not to another marriage.

THE OPPOSITE OF ART

On the Parallel between
Commerce and Bureaucracy

I once had the honor of conducting negotiations with the writer R.J. Peskens, the literary pseudonym of one of Holland's foremost post-war independent publishers. At the beginning of the 1980s, the Dutch publisher J.M. Meulenhoff, where I had just started as an apprentice, wanted to publish one of his stories in an annual anthology. The anthology was to bear the shame-lessly commercial – but for years successful – title *Goed gebun-deld – Well Collected*. The elderly Peskens was well aware that money was to be made from this venture, and he left us waiting for permission to include his story. Even the deadline set in the reminder we sent him had already expired. The entire book was in fact at the galley proof stage and nothing major could be changed. The only thing left to do was call the author and try to get his permission over the phone. So I mustered all my courage and soon had him on the line.

After explaining, at his request, why I was calling – which he knew well enough – and telling him how much we would appreciate his permission, the following conversation took place:

'Have you read the story?' he asked.

'Of course I have.'

'And wasn't it simply won-der-ful?'

'Yes, an exceptionally beautiful story.'

'And what did you find so beautiful about it?'

I leafed nervously through the galley proofs in front of me and tried in the meantime to start a sentence: 'Yes, eh, the structure… and the tone too. Magnificent.'

The author spotted the opening he had been working towards and announced with a sonorous voice: "Good. But don't you think that five hundred guilders is scandalously little for such a wonderful story?'

I obligingly explained that the fee was based on a royalty of 10% of the retail price, which was to be shared equally between the various authors and the editor, and that I didn't want to treat the other authors unfairly by making exceptions in certain cases. In short, I hoped he would agree to the publication of his story for the standard fee.

But Peskens stood his ground and wasn't about to fall for my unpolished smooth talk. His sonorous voice resounded adamantly:

'A thousand guilders!'

I protested politely that our calculations didn't permit such a payment, that this was twice the amount we had paid to the other highly respected authors, and similar irrelevant objections. He suggested we drop the story.

Desperation took hold. I was a twenty-three-year-old rookie talking on the phone to the alter ego of the most important literary publisher in post-war Netherlands. Dropping a story from the anthology, moreover, was the last thing we wanted since it simply guaranteed delays and extra costs. With these thoughts racing through my head, I pushed the envelope one last time. I admitted that the production process was at a relatively advanced stage and that I would be happy to meet him halfway if that would help us reach an agreement. To cut a long story short: a fee of seven-hundred and fifty guilders was surely enough to satisfy both parties and expedite publication of the book.

Peskens fell silent.

I thought I had done the right thing, but the silence on the other end of the line left me in doubt. Was he about to fly into a rage or explode with laughter? Had he heard my offer? Just as I was about to ask if he was still there, he barked one last time just to remind me who was the boss in our conversation: 'Seven-hundred and fifty-*one!*'

AS A PUBLISHER, GEERT VAN OORSCHOT PUT TOGETHER a remarkable catalog of Dutch literature, published a number of important collected works, and was responsible for a series of Russian translations that was and remains unparalleled in the Netherlands. At the same time, he was also a ruthless businessman and negotiator. Under the pseudonym Peskens, moreover, he was an exceptional and relatively successful prose writer. My impression is that in literary circles he preferred to expose his business side, while he was more inclined to appeal to literary arguments with his business associates (booksellers, printers, binders), thus preventing them from approaching negotiations in an exclusively commercial manner. The publishing world is familiar with these two faces – the commercial and the artistic – but few have been able to combine them with the same panache as Van Oorschot. Some publishers apply the procedure in reverse and thus incorrectly, pretending to be business-savvy in the company of businessmen, and showing off their enormous literary expertise in the company of writers.

I'M OFTEN REMINDED OF THE TWO FACES OF BUSI-nessman-litterateur Van Oorschot when I'm reflecting on the relationship between government authorities and the world of the arts, or more specifically between civil servants and art.

If you asked me to sum up the duality in which Van Oorschot was such an expert in a single word then I would say 'anti-chameleonic', a disposition I believe the art sector civil servant must also adopt, and of necessity. Dictionaries define the concept 'chameleonic' as: 'like a chameleon', 'always changing', 'unpredictable', 'unreliable' and sometimes refer to the expression 'chameleonic politics' by way of example. The art sector civil servant has to be the opposite of a chameleon in every respect. As a matter of fact, he or she can't be un-chameleonic enough. Let me explain what I mean here from three different perspectives: the administrative, the cultural-political, and the personal.

IN ADDITION TO A PLETHORA OF COLLEAGUE CIVIL SER-
vants, anyone starting work in one of the Dutch government
departments in The Hague will be confronted with the politicians he or she is expected to serve on the one hand, and
the institutions and individuals for whom government policy is
intended on the other. As they learn their trade, civil servants
are often tossed back and forth between the magnetic forces
that emanate from both domains. Sometimes novice civil servants presume that they are first and foremost the servants of
democratically elected politicians and this determines their
approach to the administrative sector in which they work. At
other times they consider themselves called to draw as much
political attention as possible to the interests of the sector for
which they are responsible.

This, of course, is an inner conflict that can lead to confusion for the novice civil servant and there is only one way
to resolve it: develop a personal professionalism whereby one
is both loyal to politics and committed to one's sector. Or, in
anti-chameleonic terms, by ensuring that you maintain your
position and responsibility in both worlds with as much visi-
bility as possible. You must never blend into the background in
whichever world you find yourself. Never blend in, always stand
out. The latter is also important in terms of internal organization. In a government department, which is programmed by its
very nature to enforce procedures, planning & control, accountability and management – while initialing every last detail as a
sign of formal approval – the art sector civil servant has to make
room for flexibility, opinion, interaction with the outside world,
and personal conviction. At the same time, the chaotic outside

world, the lobbyists, those who advocate particular causes, must always be reminded that there are transparent procedures, that responsibilities have to be met, that the democratic imperative must always have the last word even if it didn't have the first.

It's all the more difficult to learn the lesson of independent professionalism in the domain of arts management, where civil servants tend to assert their artistic affinities louder than elsewhere (something that makes them suspicious in the eyes of other civil servants, especially the finance experts and the accountants). The said lesson is also difficult to apply when it comes to formulating achievable policy goals. What exactly are the goals of dance or museum policy, and how do you formulate them in a meaningful, ambitious, workable, and accountable manner? But the lesson is equally difficult to learn in the practical sense, when one comes face to face, for example, with the creative community itself. There is always a temptation in such instances to play the chameleon, to wrap yourself in the colors of your political boss (and automatically align oneself with his or her promises and resolutions), or espouse the ideas of the cultural opinion makers (thereby placing art above politics). Helmsmanship is necessary in either direction, to avoid the Scylla of servility on the one hand, and the Charybdis of personal peculiarity on the other.

THE HYBRID POSITION OF THE ART SECTOR CIVIL SERvant also has to do with the uniqueness of the phenomenon 'cultural policy'. There are two irrefutable truths in this regard, both of which require some basic words of explanation.

First: a civilized country spends a reasonable portion of

its budget on cultural facilities for its citizens, offering them a degree of choice and facilitating personal development, opportunity to participate, and providing something to build on. The people who make these facilities real (artists, archaeologists, writers, directors, choreographers, museum curators) must be free in their artistic and cultural creativity, without having to deal with a perpetual stream of government interference. 'True freedom obeys the law,' no one would disagree, but the opposite is also true in the world of art: 'true law obeys freedom', and this applies in particular to artistic freedom.

The second irrefutable truth is that the Dutch culture budget comes from tax money distributed by the government with particular goals in mind. These goals have to be achieved, and as with every other domain of government policy, the available tax money has to be accounted for to the last eurocent. Art may be a very special phenomenon in the eyes of artists and the creative community at large, more important than water, defense, or nature reserves, but no one is obliged to ask the authorities to subsidize their cultural activities. If one does, then one has to accept that the same rules apply as they do to every other aspect of government expenditure.

It is the task of the art sector civil servant to reconcile these mutually exclusive truths and that requires the ability to switch when necessary, and in a professional and personal manner, between the two worlds in which they live and move: the world of administration and the world of art.

TO MAINTAIN THIS EXTRAORDINARY 'COMBINATION OF contradictions', the art sector civil servant must also have an

anti-chameleonic disposition at the personal level. When surrounded by politicians they will have to display not only an
understanding of political-administrative processes, but also
of art and culture. In the company of artists and the creative
community, they will have to display not only a perspective on
art and culture, but also that they are familiar with politics,
administrative processes, and public finances. In other words:
they will have to know the rules in each domain and at the same
time be able to embody the exception. One sometimes needs a
little black to allow white to be white, and at other times just
enough white to grant black its blackness. Especially when one
bears in mind that art policy is by far the most colorful policy
sector there is.

In his address to Jan Riezenkamp on March 25th, 2003, on
the occasion of the latter's retirement as Director General for
Culture and Media – a division of the Ministry of Education,
Culture, and Science – Henk van Os, the former director of
Amsterdam's Rijksmuseum, recalled a sense of being unmasked
as a pretentious big shot when he arrived at Riezenkamp's office
in a gray and gentlemanly three-piece suit to be greeted by his
host and negotiating partner in a Hawaiian shirt and sandals.
Anti-chameleonic at its very best! But Riezenkamp's personal
flair and exuberant passion for culture also embodied an inbuilt
counterbalance: he was a hard negotiator. The so-called 'good
cop' and the proverbial 'bad cop' were united in him, as many
a management team, board of directors, and sector representa-
tive was to find out over the years.

Jan Riezenkamp also managed to perfect this inimitable
duality in his personal interaction with representatives of the

cultural sector. In more formal company, for example, he liked to juggle with literary quotations and cite passages from opera libretti, while in discussions with cultural institutions he often surprised his interlocutors with references to fiscal legislation and formal funding regulations.

THIS MORE ANECDOTAL REFLECTION ON THE ANTI-chameleonic motif in the public bureaucracy surrounding the world of art and culture is in complete agreement with the two key concepts of contemporary cultural policy: autonomy and accountability.

The principle of autonomy teaches us that cultural institutions must be allowed to do their work in complete freedom, and be able to take responsibility for the social and commercial aspects of their cultural and commercial activities, without being impeded by regulatory overload and too much bureaucratic ballast on the part of the authorities nit-picking.

The principle of accountability demands that important subsidy preconditions and funding regulations are followed to the letter by the authorities in order to monitor operational functionality (the implementation of policies established by the politicians) and legality (the provision of adequate accountability for the use of subsidized funding).

ALL THINGS CONSIDERED, THERE WOULD APPEAR TO BE no fundamental difference in this regard with what one might expect of a literary publisher. They have to make sure on the one hand that writers are free to develop to the best of their ability and thus make the best possible contribution to literary culture.

On the other hand, publishers are also expected to account for their activities, providing tax authorities and shareholders with regular operational and financial reports.

The conclusion has to be that Geert van Oorschot, litterateur and savvy businessman, a man with an apparently effortless talent for remaining anti-chameleonic in both worlds, exemplifies the relationship between the civil servant and the world of art to perfection. The fact that he so evidently belonged to the private and not the public sector pales into insignificance in face of the similarities between these two anti-chameleonic attitudes.

THE DOVE FANCIER
AND THE DOCTOR

The Shoah in Facts and Stories

One of the more irritating side effects of the contemporary western personality cult is the appearance on the
back cover of predominantly English language books of other
people's opinions on the book in question but little if anything
of substance about its content. You pick up a book in the store
by a writer you've never heard of and read: 'I adored it. *The
Road to Heaven* is fantastically funny and excruciatingly wise. A
gem', or words to that effect, usually followed by a name (Jane
Brockman or Roberto Walting) you've likewise never heard
of. Those even slightly familiar with the way such recommendations are gathered by Anglo-Saxon publishers and literary
agents from their own authors will be unsurprisingly inclined to
take them with a large pinch of salt.

There are times, nevertheless, that recommendations of this sort work wonders for an unknown author. On a visit to a New York bookstore, I once picked up a book by Bernard Gotfryd entitled *Anton the Dove Fancier*, with the subtitle *And Other Tales of the Holocaust*. A mixture of unconscious respect and instinctive curiosity made me pick it up, but when I read the laudatory quotations from Oliver Sacks and Primo Levi on the book's back cover I realized it had to be something special. Both Sacks and Levi are responsible for great works of literature in which they were able to formulate the extremes of the human domain from a highly personal perspective, ultimately defined by their profession (neurologist and chemist respectively). The combined recommendation of these two authors suggested that the unfamiliar Bernard Gotfryd and his collection of stories had something significant to contribute on the area of overlap between the work of Sacks and the work of Levi, an area we might describe as 'averting the extreme' by telling stories.

My expectations were thus particularly high when I decided to purchase *Anton the Dove Fancier*, and the book itself lived up to every word of the recommendations. It begins with a description of a number of episodes in the life of a smart but sensitive boy growing up in the 1930s in the Polish provincial town of Radom, where he and his parents live in the ghetto. He manages to find a job at a photographer's studio, where he secretly makes copies of photos handed in for developing and printing by the German occupier and passes them on to the Polish resistance. He ends up in Majdanek concentration camp in the latter part of 1943 and after a period in Mauthausen and Gusen II (near Linz in Austria) he is ultimately liberated.

Soon after the war he emigrates to America, where he continues his career as a photographer, including several years working for *Newsweek*.

What I find extraordinary about these interrelated stories is that they not only reveal how Gotfryd is unsurpassed in maintaining his humanity in the midst of the indescribable, but that he also succeeds in describing the horrendous misery around him with an uncommon gentleness and purity reminiscent of Primo Levi. But the most remarkable thing about the stories in *Anton the Dove Fancier* is that the author manages to transmit the intensity and ongoing effects of his memories to the reader as a novelist would. As reader you share Gotfryd's life in the literal sense because his stories make the passage of time – the weight of what he is experiencing made heavier by time – tangible. This is genuine 'memoir literature' at its very best, literature based on memories, but also with memories themselves as subject matter: alienating, senseless, marvelous and at the same time deceptive. These stories form a self-created but virtuoso link that bridges the gulf between a life before and after the war, before and after emigration.

Not all of Gotfryd's stories deal directly with the war, but even if they have a different focus – an amorous crush, his grandmother, a stolen table, his work as a photographer, being robbed on the street – they're still about the war in one way or another. In retrospect, the early stories are clearly a prelude to the occupation and the formation of the Radom ghetto, while the remaining stories are defined by the loss and rediscovery of people and memories. Gotfryd started to write down these stories about his life after a working visit to Poland, when he was commissioned by *Newsweek* to cover the papal visit in 1983. Forty years had passed since Gotfryd last saw the country and city of his birth, and it is perfectly possible that the decision to write down his memories after such an elapse of time contributed to their exceptional weight, to the tangible durability of his descriptions of the past. What would he have written if he – like Primo Levi – had started to note down his dreadful experiences immediately after the war in 1946-1947? A stupid question perhaps, since we can assume that what Bernard Gotfryd needed in 1946-1947 wasn't writing stories. He needed rather to 'avert the extreme' by *not* writing stories.

IT IS AN INTERESTING EXERCISE TO EXAMINE THE STO-ries of Bernard Gotfryd, his memories ripened retrospectively over a long period of time, side by side with an autobiographical book about the Shoah that came into my possession around the same time, a book in which Gotfryd's retrospective distance is completely absent. The book is called *Ein jüdischer Arzt-Kalender. Durch Westerbork und Bergen-Belsen nach Tröbitz. Konzentrationslager-Tagebuch 1943-1945 – A Jewish Physician's Almanac. Through Westerbork and Bergen-Belsen to Tröbitz. Concentration Camp Diary 1943-1945* . It was written by Felix Hermann Oestreicher and edited by his daughter Maria Goudsblom-Oestreicher with Erhard Roy Wiehn. The book contains daily penciled entries written with the help of a magnifying glass in a doctor's four-by-six-inch pocket diary between November 1st, 1943, and May 21st, 1945, by a Bohemian born doctor who had moved to the Netherlands before the war. The exceptionally limiting circumstances under which Oestreicher kept his diary made deciphering his often cryptic short-hand notes an enormous task, and to designate it a labor of love would still be a euphemism. In her foreword, Oestreicher's daughter states her presumption that her father probably intended to base his memoirs on these extremely compact and factual notes but never had the opportunity. He died on June 9th, 1946, of typhoid fever a month after being liberated from Bergen-Belsen, and a little more than a week after his wife succumbed to the same illness. His two daughters took the diary back to the Netherlands where they stored it with care in a cupboard. It remained unread for fifty years.

Oestreicher's daily entries could not have been plainer. There is evidence of minimal reflection, a result of the circumstances in which he found himself and the limited size of the diary itself. He observed everyday facts following a fixed pattern: what he was given to eat, how often he visited the toilet and when, how he and his family had slept, how many patients he had treated, where and how he was able to shave, times at which a roll call was taken and at what hour the air-raid siren sounded, the deaths of the day, keywords on the weather, what he was reading, and other mundane activities such as card games.

I read this book from cover to cover, but in hindsight the word 'read' is inadequate. It's not a book in the conventional sense, but a transcript edition of what might best be described as a white-hot clay tablet, scrawled with words in a language that was only to be deciphered with extreme patience and precision. These everyday observations, moreover, are so close to the facts they describe that they're barely more than the facts themselves and as such they are nothing new. What they *are* is personal, highly personal, in the sense that they are observed from the perspective of a person who experienced everything hour by hour, a doctor (*'Ich wil gerne Arzt bleiben* – I want to stay a doctor,' Oestreicher noted on April 14th, 1944, in Bergen-Belsen) who wrote prescriptions for survival to himself, as it were. In the middle of his notes we also find nineteen poems, which were published separately a few years later in a German/Dutch edition entitled *Nachher/Naderhand - Afterwards.* In one of the poems, similarly plain and concise, the simple yet devastating lines articulate the same sensation that overcomes you when you see pictures or films of the persecution of Jews: *'Wir sind schon lange gestorben, / Wir wissen es nur nicht.* We died a long time ago, / We just didn't know it.'

In spite of the unadorned and factual character of Oestreicher's diary, its publication as a book that you can read and will want to read to the last page – and a book that stays with you forever – is due in the first instance to the foreword, introduction, and epilogue written by his daughter Maria Goudsblom-Oestreicher. With equal measures of intensity and conciseness, she manages to place the life and death of her parents in a biographical and personal context, intermingled with her own memories as a young girl of the profoundly tragic course of events. The few pages she dedicates at the beginning of the book to the many years she had the diary in her possession without being able to decipher its contents, and the pages at the end of the book in which she describes the death of her parents, betray a rare musicality and savoir-vivre, face to face – albeit across a gulf of fifty years – with the darkest pages in her own life.

A PERHAPS INAPPROPRIATE, BUT NEVERTHELESS interesting question is: which of these two books best represents the essence of the Shoah as a human experience? The narrative depiction written by Gotfryd forty years after the event or Oestreicher's short-hand chronicle of everyday facts written at the moment itself? In his magnificent study *Vervolging, vernietiging, literatuur* – *Persecution, Extermination, Literature*, Leiden based literary theorist and essayist S. Dresden endeavors to locate belletristic literature on the persecution of the Jews vis-à-vis pure, factual testimonies on the same topic. His study focuses on the relationship between the two categories, and in particular on the issue of the moral and historical legitimacy of the former and the artistic worth of the latter. In other words: should we make literature with genocide as its subject? And vice versa: should we judge such a shocking factual account in aesthetic, literary terms?

As far as I can see, the crux of Dresden's book is to be found in a highly personal passage in which he comes to the conclusion that the factual and immediate report – no matter how important in historiographical terms – has to take second place to the narrative imagination's capacity to do justice to reality, to make the incredible credible. With this conviction at its core, Dresden's essay emerges as one of the most fundamental – and indeed most moving – defenses of literature I have ever encountered. In the context of our present dilemma, Dresden's conviction would imply that the literary stories written in retrospect by Gotfryd should be rated higher than Oestreicher's factual notes written as events took place. The literature of the imagination thus wins out over the historical facts scribbled on the spot.

But should the evident difference between these difficult to compare categories necessarily lead us to opt for one and not the other? Perhaps we might argue that the events themselves constitute the first dimension, their immediate recording the second, and the memories and stories written down after time has passed the third. These three dimensions thus complement one another and together represent as complete a picture as possible of past reality. It might also liberate me as a reader from a moral dilemma that should not be subjugated to the fine points of the relationship between historiography and literature. Comparing can be interesting, but we should not let it become an end in itself.

ACKNOWLEDGMENTS

Unless otherwise stated, the essays published in the present volume originally appeared in the Dutch journal *De Gids*. Where necessary, they were revised and supplemented for republication. A list of sources used in each essay is provided below.

APPLES AND ORANGES

Peter Burke, *History and Social Theory* (Cambridge, 1992).

Epistolario di Silvio Pellico – Letters of Silvio Pellico (Milan, 1869).

Peter Gay, *Freud. A Life for Our Time* (New York, 1988).

Rob Riemen, *De eeuwige terugkeer van het fascisme – The Eternal Return of Fascism* (Amsterdam, 2010).

A TALE OF TWO SEAS

Predrag Matvejević, *Mediterranean: A Cultural Landscape* (Berkeley, 1994).

THE CLEVERINGA SCALE

Herstel? der universiteiten (December 1945), a publication of the *Interacademiale Contact van Studenten-Tekenaars*.

C.J.H. Jansen and D. Venema, 'De 26 november-rede van prof. mr. R.P. Cleveringa (1894-1980)' in *Nederlands Juristenblad* 18 (2006).

Corjo Jansen, in association with Derk Venema, *De Hoge Raad en de Tweede Wereldoorlog. Recht en rechtsbeoefening in de jaren 1930-1950* (Amsterdam, 2011).

P.J. van Koppen and J. ten Cate, *De Hoge Raad in persoon: benoemingen in de Hoge Raad der Nederlanden 1838-2002* (Deventer, 2003).

Ingo Müller, *Furchtbare Juristen. Die unbewältigte Vergangenheit unserer Justiz* (Munich, 1987).

Kees Schuyt and Ineke Sluiter (eds.), *Cleveringa's koffer. Recht, vrijheid en verantwoordelijkheid. Een selectie uit de 26-novemberredes aan de Universiteit Leiden, 1940-2010* (Leiden, 2010).

'Justiz-Ranking in der EU. Unterschiedliche Verfahrensdauer', *Neue Zürcher Zeitung*, March 30th, 2013.

HAMLET AND TELEMACHUS

Homer, *Odyssey* (translated by Robert Fagles, 1996).

Irene J.F. de Jong, *In betovering gevangen. Aspecten van Homerus' vertelkunst* (Amsterdam, 1992).

William Shakespeare, *Hamlet* (edited by T.B.J. Spencer, London, 1980).

THE QUESTIONABLE PROBLEM

Myriam Anissimov, *Primo Levi. Tragedy of an Optimist* (translated by Steve Cox, London, 1998).

Marc Etkind, *Or Not to Be. A Collection of Suicide Notes* (New York, 1997).

Primo Levi, 'Hatching the Cobra' in *The Mirror Maker. Stories and Essays* (translated by Raymond Rosenthal, London, 1990).

Ivan Morris, *The Nobility of Failure* (London, 1975).

Richard O'Neill, *Suicide Squads. The Men and Machines of World War II Special Operations* (London, 1999).

Maurice Pinguet, *Voluntary Death in Japan* (translated by Rosemary Morris, Cambridge, 1993).

NAPOLEON AND ME IN ALKMAAR

[originally published in Kees de Bakker (ed.), *Hier begint de victorie. Schrijvers over Alkmaar* (Schoorl, 2008)].

E.H.P. Cordfunke, 'Napoleon in Alkmaar' in *Alkmaars Jaarboekje 1967*.

G.N.M. Vis *et al.*, *Geschiedenis van Alkmaar* (Zwolle, 2007).

Jorge Luis Borges, 'The Aleph' in *The Aleph and Other Stories* (translated by Andrew Hurley, London, 2000).

THREE WAYS TO BECOME A JEW

[originally published in *Armada. Tijdschrift voor wereldliteratuur* 16 (2010), 60].

David Brauner, *Post-War Jewish Fiction: Ambivalence, Self-Explanation and Transatlantic Connections* (New York, 2001).

Philip Davis, *Bernard Malamud. A Writer's Life* (New York, 2007).

Laura Z. Hobson, *Gentleman's Agreement* (New York, 1947).

Bernard Malamud, *The Assistant* (New York, 1957).

Arthur Miller, *Focus* (New York, 1945).

www.vcn.bc.ca/outlook/library/articles/secular_humanism/05j_ LauraHobson.htm

THE SHIP AND THE CARGO

[originally published in *Armada. Tijdschrift voor wereldliteratuur* 14 (2008), 50].

Arthur van Schendel, *Het fregatschip Johanna Maria* (Amsterdam, 1930). *The 'Johanna Maria'* (translated by Brian W. Downs, London, 1935).

A FALSE DAWN

[originally published in *Armada. Tijdschrift voor wereldliteratuur* 18 (2012), 68].

Oscar Wilde, *The Complete Letters* (edited by Merlin Holland and Rupert Hart-Davis, London, 2000).

NEUTRALITY VERSUS ENGAGEMENT

[originally published in Yra van Dijk (ed.), *Geloof mij Uw oprechte en dankbare vriend – Believe Me Your Sincere and Grateful Friend*, on the occasion of the retirement of Prof. Dr M.T.C. Mathijsen-Verkooijen (www.dbnl. org, 2009)].

Bertus Aafjes, *Verzamelde gedichten* (Amsterdam, 1990).

Jef Last, *Brieven uit Spanje – Letters From Spain* (Amsterdam, 1936) and *De Spaanse tragedie – The Spanish Tragedy* (Amsterdam, 1938, 1962).

THE CONSCIOUSNESS OF ITALY

[originally published in Jörg Remé, *Het bewustzijn van Italië - The Consciousness of Italy* (Amsterdam, 2009)].

Susanne Cassirer Bernfeld, 'Freud en de archeologie' in *Psychoanalytische perspectieven* 24 (2006): pp. 117-137.

Sigmund Freud, *The Complete Letters of Sigmund Freud to Wilhelm Fliess* (Cambridge, 1986), *Studies on Hysteria* (translated and edited by James Strachey, New York, 2009), *Civilization and Its Discontents* (translated by James Strachey, New York, 1989) and *Constructions in Analysis* (1937).

James Money, *Capri. Island of Pleasure* (London, 1986).

Heinrich Schliemann, *Ilios. The City and the Country of the Trojans* (Salem, 1989).

Michael Shortland, 'Powers of Recall. Sigmund Freud's Partiality for the Prehistoric' (*Australasian Historical Archeology* 11 [1993]), pp. 3-20.

A DANCING FATHER

[originally published in *Vrij Nederland*, July 28th, 2001].

Bliss Broyard, *My Father, Dancing* (New York, 1999) and *One Drop. My Father's Hidden Life* (New York, 2007).

Henry Louis Gates, Jr., 'The Passing of Anatole Broyard' in *Thirteen Ways of Looking at a Black Man* (New York, 1997).

Philip Roth, 'Open Letter to Wikipedia', *The New Yorker*, September 7th, 2012.

THE LATERVEER BOX

With gratitude to Anneke van Veen for helping identify a number of the photos and their makers.

NOT THE BARS BUT THE DOOR

Roland Barthes, *La préparation du roman I et II. Cours et séminaires au Collège de France (1978-1979 et 1979-1980)* (Paris, 2003).

Joseph Brodsky, 'Less Than One' in *Less Than One. Selected Essays* (New York, 1986)

Alain Buisine, *Proust. Samedi 27 novembre 1909* (Paris, 1991).

W.B. Carnochan, 'The Literature of Confinement' in *The Oxford History of the Prison. The Practice of Punishment in Western Society* (Oxford, 1998).

Jan van Luxemburg, Mieke Bal, Willem G. Weststeijn, *Inleiding in de literatuurwetenschap* (Muiderberg, 1982).

Douglas Murray, *Bosie. A Biography of Lord Alfred Douglas* (New York, 2000).

Tony Perrottet, 'Why Writers Belong Behind Bars', *New York Times*, July 20th, 2011.

THE VILLAGE AND THE WORLD
[originally published in the Flemish journal *Ons Erfdeel* 49 (2006), pp. 761-763].

Lieve Joris, *The Rebel's Hour* (translated by Liz Waters, New York, 2008)

ERNEST DOWSON AND FRANCIS DONNE
[originally published in *Raster* 99 (2002)].

Jad Adams, *Madder Music, Stronger Wine. The Life of Ernest Dowson, Poet and Decadent* (London, 2000).

Desmond Flower and Henry Maas, *The Letters of Ernest Dowson* (Rutherford, 1967).

Mark Longaker, *Ernest Dowson* (London, 1944).

Victor Plarr, *Ernest Dowson 1888-1897* (New York, 1914).

THE BIG PICTURE AND THE SMALL
[originally published in *De Groene Amsterdammer* 127 (2003), 12].

Henk van Os, 'Het grote verhaal in de kunstgeschiedenis' in *De Groene Amsterdammer* 127 (2003), 10.

THE MARCHIONESS TOOK THE NINE O'CLOCK TRAIN
[originally published in *Raster* 96 (1996)].

Paul Valéry, *Cahiers 1-29* (Paris, 1957-1961) and *Cahiers I & II* (edited by Judith Robinson-Valéry, Paris, 1973-1974).

PHOTOGRAPHY AND AUTOBIOGRAPHY
[originally published in *Vrij Nederland*, May 5th, 2007].

Rudy Kousbroek, *Opgespoorde wonderen – Recovered Miracles* (Amsterdam, 2010).

TO WED OR NOT TO WED

[originally published in *Armada* 13 (2007), 47].

James Atlas, *Delmore Schwartz. The Life of an American Poet* (New York, 1977).

Saul Bellow, *Humboldt's Gift* (New York, 1975).

Anatole Broyard, *Kafka Was the Rage* (New York, 1993).

Richard McDougall, *Delmore Schwartz* (New York, 1974).

Arthur Miller, *Timebends: A Life* (New York, 1987).

Delmore Schwartz, *In Dreams Begin Responsibilities and Other Stories* (New York, 1937, 1978).

THE OPPOSITE OF ART

[originally published in *Tirade* 47 (2003), pp. 8-14].

THE DOVE FANCIER AND THE DOCTOR

S. Dresden, *Persecution, Extermination, Literature* (translated by Henry Schogt, Toronto, 1995).

Bernard Gotfryd, *Anton the Dove Fancier and Other Tales of the Holocaust* (Baltimore, 2000).

Felix Hermann Oestreicher (edited by Maria Goudsblom-Oestreicher with Erhard Roy Wiehn), *Ein jüdischer Arzt-Kalender. Durch Westerbork und Bergen-Belsen nach Tröbitz. Konzentrationslager-Tagebuch 1943-1945* (Konstanz, 2000).

Felix Oestreicher, *Nachher/Naderhand. Lagergedichte/Kampgedichten* (translated by Ton Naaijkens, Enschede/Doetinchem, 2013).

Maarten Asscher (°1957) studied law and Assyriology at Leyden University in the Netherlands. He started his career in literary publishing in 1980 and became the Dutch publisher of writers such as Carlos Fuentes, Primo Levi, Amos Oz and Wisława Szymborska. In 2004, after six years as a cultural policy advisor at the Dutch Ministry of Education, Culture and Science, he became an independent bookseller. He is presently director and co-owner of the Athenaeum Bookshop in Amsterdam. He has written and published poetry, short stories and novellas, a novel and several books of essays, among them an aquatic history of the Netherlands

(*H₂Olland. A Quest for the Sources of the Netherlands*). Most of his books have also appeared in German translation. He has translated poetry by such diverse poets as Paul Valéry, Albrecht Haushofer and Fernando Pessoa. *Apples and Oranges. In Praise of Comparisons* was originally published in Dutch in 2013. This is his first book to be translated into English. Maarten Asscher lives in Amsterdam with his wife and daughter. He has two adult daughters from a previous marriage.

Translator Brian Doyle-Du Breuil (°1956) studied Hebrew and Hebrew Bible in Dublin and the University of Leuven (Belgium), where he presently teaches courses in biblical Hebrew and the Hebrew Bible. In addition to his university work, he has translated a variety of genres from Dutch into English over a period of more than twenty years, including several academic monographs, novels, literary non-fiction and poetry.

CPSIA information can be obtained at www.ICGtesting.com
Printed in the USA
LVOW08s2245240315

431839LV00001BA/1/P